BECOME THE TYPE OF PERSON THAT GETS THE GOAL

The Simple Ways You Can Start Working Toward Your Dream Life

Cayleb Pletos

YOUR JOURNEY

On your journey to success, you will encounter many different obstacles. The path is not easy, but it is worth it. This book will help to give you the knowledge to face these challenges and propel you on your path to success. The journey of bettering one's self is the greatest journey of them all. Enjoy the ride.

TO MY MOTHER AND FATHER

I cannot thank you enough for your everlasting love and support. I will always seek to expand on the knowledge you have given me. I love you.

CONTENTS

INTRODUCTION

There's motivation all around us in the modern world. It's not hard to stumble upon a motivational video or podcast. Many of us are motivated directly by the music that we listen to on a daily basis. Sometimes there is a deeper meaning to it. Many of you are motivated because you need to provide for your loved ones. You want to provide for your significant other, children, or parents. You want to make a change in your life and the world. This is what gets you up in the morning.

Unfortunately, many of us are confused on this path to living our dream life. We struggle to bridge the gap between wanting to be great and being great humans. Once we are motivated, we end up overwhelmed and giving up. The path to success often seems complex. We look at successful people and think, "how in the world did they do all that?" But like anything, it can be broken down into many small actions that are consistently repeated. That's it. Success is the product of a cycle, and while everyone's path looks different, these rules still hold true.

Once you get the ball rolling, it's not as complex as it may seem. It's very hard. It will require tremendous amounts of strength. But success is not complex. The more you learn about the process, the easier it gets, and the better you will become. This book aims to help you bridge the gap between the idea of changing your life to living your dream life by providing tips, tricks, and stories of overcoming challenges. We will break down every aspect of your life, revamp it, and push you to achieve your individual goals. They may be financial, health-related, or relationship based; the methods discussed will be versatile, and all will assist you in crafting your dream life.

If you picked up this book, that means you have a desire to change. Something inside you wants more.

Maybe you fear being average, or maybe you just have something to prove. Whatever the reason, I'm glad you're here. The first step to change is being honest with yourself and admitting that a change needs to be made. Congrats on the completion of the first step.

I wanted to start this book off by saying that you have the power to do anything you put your mind to. The power to become a millionaire, the power to become a star athlete, and the ability to push yourself to the limits in the name of self-betterment. Regardless of your race, current financial situation, home life, or of the ways people have done you wrong. You have total power and control to change your life and live at a caliber to which you once thought unimaginable.

In order to achieve your dream life, you must stop at nothing, and I mean absolutely nothing in order to get there. You can't worry about other people's opinions. You can't worry about the hours on end that it will take to achieve this lifestyle, and you can't be afraid to go against societal standard and social norms.

So, you watched a few motivational videos, or you're stuck in life, and you want to make a change. Now what?

This book is here to help you understand where to start, at any point in your life, to prime your current situation for success.

Answer this. Have you honestly been giving your life all that you can from relationships to finances to inspiring others and everywhere in-between? No? Then it is time to make a change that your future self, your family, and future generations will thank you for.

This book is for those who don't feel right in their current situation. They struggle to figure out what it is, but something inside them doesn't like how their life is. They feel like they have greatness inside of them, and they feel like they want to change, but they're lost and don't know what to do. This book is for the person overwhelmed with the idea of changing their lives for the better. This book is for a person of any age and any place in life. Someone who knows they want more out of life and know there's got to be a way to live the dream life.

Maybe you stumbled upon this book, or maybe someone recommended it to you. Maybe you are lost and don't know where to turn. This book will help you increase your self-awareness and craft your vision. Show the steps that many others have taken to succeed in their own lives. Although each person's situation is different, how we overcome challenges and push for a better life doesn't vary a lot from one success story to another. Everyone has followed many core values and principles on the path to success. This book will help you better understand how so many people have changed their lives. So many average people have transformed their lives, and you can too.

GETTING STARTED

Self Confidence

Self-confidence is the root of all great things. You'll never do anything great in your life unless you believe in yourself. Truly believe in yourself. You cannot go about the situations in life thinking, "oh, I might pass this test" or "maybe I could make $1 million". If you don't believe in yourself, then who will? If I wanted to get a 4.0 GPA, then I tell myself I will get a 4.0. I am going to succeed because I am a winner, and winners win. If I am not confident that I will achieve my goal, then I will not. I'm sure you've heard it before, but a quote by Confucius says "he who says he can and he who says he can't are both usually right". If you truly believe in yourself, you will achieve great things, but if you do not, you will most likely fail.

There is a lot of psychology behind the self-confidence it takes to be successful. A great example of this work is the book "Think and Grow Rich" by Napoleon Hill. This book states that if you repeatedly push an action onto yourself, it will become second nature. Let me explain. If you wake up every day and repeatedly look in the mirror and tell yourself, "I will not give up,", then that saying will become imbedded into your sub conscious. Your mind and body will start to truly believe that you will not give up, therefore, you will begin to adopt the characteristics of determination.

It is essential to be confident IN YOUR WORK. When you say "I am the best," you set this standard for yourself. The most successful people all do this. This isn't just a lousy scheme to sound cocky or like you're trying to pull others down. This should only be used to try and push yourself up and hold yourself to the highest expectations to achieve your greatest goals. Don't get the two mixed up. Being cocky and confident is not the same thing. Imagine if your favorite author never dared to believe they could write. They would never create amazing work. If you can believe it, you can turn it into your reality. I know that sounds very cliché and sounds like a poster that you would see in the high school classroom. But to be honest, it's 100% accurate. Self-confidence is your base and your grounding.

Convincing yourself that you can do something is the first step. And if you haven't convinced yourself, then you will not achieve it. So how do we convince ourselves? By proving our worth. By constantly showing up for ourselves and earning our confidence.

A ho-hum attitude towards success will produce mediocre results. Repeating the simple words to yourself, "I can do it," will work wonders. Learning how to talk to yourself and pick yourself up is a skill that, once mastered, will pay you dividends. Your self-confidence and mind can push your body beyond its physical potential.

Here's the non-sugar coated, straight-to-the-point summery. You will achieve nothing if you don't have the bottom line confidence in yourself, which is necessary for success. You are stuck with your mind and body for the rest of your life. Once you master your relationship with yourself, there are no limits to what you can do.

This is Manageable

Success isn't some crazy magical state of being that only happens to extremely rare and special people. They didn't rub a magic lamp and get three wishes granted. They are regular people who consistently followed steps that took them to their goals and beyond. True success is in all of us; it really is possible to live your dream life.

If you form habits and follow steps that other successful people have followed, you will get to a spot in life similar to them. Success is not something that happens instantly. Get rich quick schemes are not real. Sometimes it may look like someone is an "overnight success," but I can promise you that their overnight success took years to achieve. Success is the sum of many small actions done every day for a long period. It's just the repetition of bettering yourself. You get a little better every day. Day by day, it doesn't seem like much of an improvement. But, you will look back and realize how much ground you have covered and be astonished. Anyone can do a few small things every day. Why not you?

There's no reason to be intimidated by the thought of success. There is so much knowledge on the topic available at your fingertips either on the internet, in books, or through other successful people. Getting started is the hardest part. After you have found your direction, combine it with the proper routine and faith, and you are sure to make it.

Aiming High

Aiming high is very important. Whatever your goals are, don't sell yourself short on your potential. If you're shooting to make $100,000 per year, why not double that and shoot for $200,000? We can always push farther. You're capable of great things. Yes, it may be hard, but the farther you push, the more you will get done. Think of it like this, if you aim for the $200,000 per year, but you fall short and only get $150,000 per year, you have still achieved $50,000 more than you would have if you shot low. Shoot for the moon; if you miss, you still end up in the stars.

For many reasons, it is important to seek success in different areas of your life. I believe people should have goals that touch on different categories in their lives. I usually separate my goals into four categories. Remember that this may change depending on what I want to accomplish. The categories are business, investments, health, and education.

I run a small business YouTube channel; I'll talk more about that later, but I have certain business-specific goals that I want to hit. I also have investment-related goals. For example, I want to purchase my first rental property. I believe it is important for all of us to set ourselves up financially, and I have many goals related to my financial achievements.

I also have many goals related to my health. This can be both mental health and physical health. Both mental and physical health is extremely important in life, and they can help you achieve other goals. Some of these health-related goals I have are to improve my weight lifting numbers and reach a certain body weight goal. I also have many education-related goals. Over the years, these have changed as I have graduated college and moved on to different types of education. But, one of my big education goals this year is to read ten self-help or personal growth related books.

I will create a large list of goals in these categories every year. As the year goes on, I will use that as a road map to achieving what I want. I look at this sheet to bring me back when I get off course. Sometimes I need to adjust these goals a little and change them slightly. Maybe I decide to pivot and go in a different direction in my business or a project I'm working on.

My yearly goals are always pretty high. There are lots of goals that I want to achieve. Realistically, I won't hit all of them this year. For example, I broke my leg this year. This put me way behind on some of my fitness goals. Sometimes in life, we run into problems and setbacks. Sometimes things take longer than we expect.

But I aim high to try and accomplish as much as I can. I know that aiming for a target will point me in the right direction. Even if that target is far away.

Goals

Everyone has something that they can do to improve their life. Every one of us has a dream or a goal deep inside. Even if we don't know it. Take a long look at your life. Where do you think you can improve? What would your ideal day look like? Your ideal body, bank account, and job? What improvements could you make in life to feel happier? Maybe you want to lose weight or start a business. Maybe you had a dream job when you were young. What did your ideal life look like before you put limitations on yourself?

Having a goal is the first step to changing your life. After all, you cannot achieve an outcome if you don't know what that outcome is. How are you going to hit a target you can't see? A goal without a plan of action and a measurable timeline is just a wish. There are many acronyms like the SMART goal, to help you plan your achievements. You have probably heard of something like this before, but it is still worth reviewing.

SMART stands for specific, measurable, achievable, realistic, and timely. These are the guidelines and rules that you should use when creating a goal for yourself. Let's go through each one of these individually. I'll try to make this as simple and easy as possible.

Specific: A specific goal gives you an exact goal, numerically if possible, to aim for. Let's use the example of losing weight. If your goal is to lose weight, don't make your goal "I want to lose weight". This is not specific enough. It gives you no real target to aim for. A better goal is "I want to lose 30 pounds". Pretty easy, it just helps you actually identify your goal more.

Measurable: Your goal should have a measurable timeline so that you can track it along the way. Continuing with our weight example, your measurable goal should be "I want to lose 5 pounds of fat per month," and then track yourself along the way to see how you progress.

Achievable: Your short-term goal should be between sluggish and unachievable. This goal should stretch you to preform, but it can't be so big that you don't even try. If you made a goal to become a millionaire in two days, that's not realistic. Unless you actually have the means. Your goal needs to challenge you to become better. You must have the knowledge to achieve the goal or the motivation to go out and find the knowledge you need. I am all for the optimism, just on a realistic timeline.

Realistic: I would encourage you to aim high, but you need to come out of the gate realistic as well. Back to our weight example, you cannot give yourself the goal of losing 30 pounds in one week because it is just purely not realistic. It's also just not healthy. Succeed the right way and progress the right way. Giving yourself an unrealistic goal can be too intimidating and cause you to be too discouraged. So much that you don't even try.

Timely: I highly encourage you to have a timeline for your goal as well. This means setting your goal up to get the ball rolling quickly and keep things moving. I usually come up with yearly goals and then break them down into a relative timeline. Things change along the way, but the relative goal remains the same.

Example of a smart goal: here is an example of a complete smart goal formatted properly. I will lose 30 pounds in the next 6 months. I will do this by going to the gym every day and eating properly. I will lose a minimum of 5 pounds a month. I will weigh myself every morning at 8 am and track my results.

Now you know how to format a proper goal for yourself. So, what should you do with this goal? WRITE IT DOWN! Just purely the activity of writing your goal down will increase the chances of you achieving it. Once you have this goal well formatted and written down, you should put this goal somewhere you will see it every day. Perhaps right above your bed so that you see it every morning after you wake up and every night you go to sleep. Another great place is the lock screen or background of your phone. Many of us go on our phones more often than we would like to admit. Seeing this goal every day will help you to think about it more, as well as help to keep you motivated when you feel like quitting. Perhaps you get home from a long day at work, and think about building that business, but you decide to call it a night and lay in bed. You look up, and your goal is staring you in the face, saying, "are you really going to sleep? You have work to do".

Being a success is not achieved after one goal. When you complete your first goal, set another goal, a bigger goal. When you have conquered one area of your life, tackle another. This is a lifelong journey that you are about to embark on. It's never over. You should always strive to be better and to achieve more than you have before. To help more people, to inspire more people, to change the lives of more people, whatever your goal is.

Champions never quit. Even after they win, they go for the next victory. Enjoy the grind and enjoy the chasing of dreams. Fall in love with the journey and be obsessed with the process of becoming great. If you love the chase, it is that much easier to keep going once the going gets tough. That makes it so much easier to accomplish your dreams.

Believe and Have Faith

In order to achieve something then, you must fully 100% believe it can happen. Put your mind to it and stop at nothing to make that thing happen. The world opens up when you trust the process and believe in yourself.

Trust really helps to bring me back when I'm at a low point. Sometimes when life is on your back, it's hard to believe. In those dark times, I look to trust. I trust myself and the methods I have in place to change my life. I may not FEEL good, but I trust the advice of others. I believe my mentors know what they are talking about and trust in them.

I know it sounds corny, but you really do need to believe in yourself. If you don't believe in yourself, then who will? Your dreams are no one else's responsibility but your own, and YOU are the only one who can make them happen. During the hard nights and through the challenging tasks, remember your faith. Remember that you not only trust yourself but also owe it to yourself to do whatever it takes to accomplish your goals.

The definition of faith is "complete trust or confidence in someone or something". To succeed to your fullest potential, you must have complete trust and confidence in yourself. Trust that if you follow the habits of those before you, you will breed the same results as those before you. Success is the equivalent of the daily work that we put in through our habits compounded over time.

I Don't Care Who You Are, Do What You Love

I know that you have always heard from a young age to "do what you love" or "find a job that you love". But there really is some truth to this. If you can find true purpose in your actions, you can find the will to go on. Even when times are tough, please, for your own good, do something with your life that you actually enjoy doing. This sounds like simple advice, but surprisingly, most people do not do this. They stay in a job they hate, stay in a relationship they don't like or keep up on habits that don't make them happy.

Most people can't wait for the week to be over because the only enjoyment they get is on those two days of the weekend, Saturday and Sunday. If you are not excited about your day every day, then you're living your life wrong. You have full control over your career choice, friend choices, and major life choices.

People have this belief that you need to choose a career that you love or you can choose to make money. In the world we live in, this is simply not the case. The internet provides an even playing field for all people, regardless of race, religion, or age, an equal chance to make as much money as they want doing what they love to do.

If you do what you love, you can work hours on end for your passion. If you do what you love, you can stay up through the night without a second thought. If you do what you love, you can wake up at 4 am off of 3 hours of sleep and jump out of bed with a smile on your face. If you do what you love, nothing will stand in your way of accomplishing your dreams.

My father told me that you just know the answer to some things in life too. He told me that within weeks of dating my mom that he wanted to marry her. When you stumble upon that dream or that passion, whatever it may be. You will know without a doubt in your mind that it is what you want to do for the rest of your life. You cannot hide your passion. Here's the story of how I found my passion for entrepreneurship, to show you how sudden and how it can come out of nowhere.

It was the middle of my high school sophomore year and the week during midterms in January. I was out to lunch with my mother at Wendy's. As I was eating my chicken sandwich and drinking my orange soda, we started to talk about what I wanted to do with my life. Before this, I had thought of many things, from being a mechanic to joining the military, to being a paleontologist. Pretty much about any career choice I could think of. I don't exactly know what it was in this conversation that got me, but she started to explain to me her experiences in the corporate world. Something sparked, something turned, I don't know how it happened, but I immediately concluded that I needed to change my life, and push myself to be the best possible person I can be. I need to figure out what I am going to do with my life.

I knew it would be somewhere in business, and as a 15-year-old, I decided to push full steam ahead onto my schoolwork and my life in general to better myself. I wanted to hold a very high-paid job in a prestigious position in corporate America. Later that year, I started to think, "why wait until after college? Why not start now?" So, I decided to be my own boss and, through the inspiration of others, started my own business. I worked a lot with flipping products. I would flip anything that I could get my hands on. I did all of this while holding jobs at various pizzerias. This is where I got my first taste of real entrepreneurship.

In my senior year of high school, I went through a co-op program which landed me a position in the financial sector of my city governmental offices. I was surrounded by lots of very nice people and very great circumstances. This was my first exposure to office life. There was only one downfall; I absolutely hated it. There was no way that I would be sitting at a desk working for somebody else for the rest of my life. Over the years, my business has changed and evolved. I've failed at many different things and eventually landed on what I do today.

Doing what you love does require balance, though. You will probably need to combine your passion with something that makes money in order to create a business out of it. Maybe you love to cook. You could start selling your meals, open a restaurant, write a cook book, or start a cooking YouTube channel. See how all these things combine your passion for cooking with something that brings in cash. There is absolutely no reason why anyone should feel forced to stay in a job they hate or live a lifestyle they don't enjoy. Not today.

Nothing is More Important

Why does all of this matter? Why should you even give this dream life thing a shot? I want to start by saying this. You have the potential to do anything. Forget about what the outside world tells you for just a second. You can do anything you set your mind to. You can accomplish any goal. You are capable of so much more than you even realize. You only get one life. You're not getting any younger, and time isn't slowing down. Don't you want to live this life to the fullest? Don't you want to see what happens if you just gave something our all?

I want you to really think about your life. It really is the most important thing that you have. It is also so valuable to the people around you. Your life has allowed you to help others and make this world a better place. How do you want your future to look? Everything in life is tough, and we must suffer either way. You can suffer the pain of discipline and hard work. That will bring you to your goal. Or, you can suffer the pain of not trying at all. I don't want you to look back 15 years from now, stuck in a job you hate and overweight with no money. That is suffering too. You must suffer either way. Choose your suffering.

If not for yourself, do it for those around you. Work hard to provide for your children. Work hard so that you can retire your parents. Work hard so you can spend more free time with those you love. How do you expect to provide for your family if you don't push yourself? How do you expect to help those in need and give back to the community if you can't even take the time to work on yourself?

Set the standard and be a good example for the people around you. Be the inspiration someone else needs to take that step in their life. There is no downside to following your dreams and living your best life. You can help others, teach others, inspire others, and make a positive change in the world.

MOTIVATION

Design Your Dream Life

In order to achieve your dream life, you need to know what that looks like. Take the time to design your dream life. If you could have anything in the world, anything that you ever wanted, think of what that would look like. Write it down. What would your ideal body be like, your financial situation be like, your relationship situation be like, and how happy would you be? Create the ideal life regardless of what it takes to get there, right down your dream life, and envision this. See yourself in this life and imagine how you would feel. Do you like the way you feel? Would you be proud to live this life? Would you be proud to tell someone what you do for a living in your ideal life? Think about your sense of achievement after reaching your ideal outcome.

You need to have a clear picture of your dream life and the goals that drive your success. It's ridiculous to think you can hit a target you can't see. You need to be very specific. Most people will create a goal like "I want to be rich". That's a terrible goal because it's not measurable, there's no timeframe, it's not specific, and you don't have a plan to get there. A goal without a plan is just a wish. In order to create a proper goal, you need to set a measurable value specific to what exactly you want. You need to develop a plan to get there. Track yourself along the way. What are you doing daily to bring you closer to your dream life?

Once you have designed this dream life, you must picture yourself living it. You need to be able to feel the happiness that your dream life will bring you. Really let your imagination run wild. See the ideal body. Smell the interior of your dream car. Imagine tasting the best food money can buy. Imagine never stressing about money again. How would you feel after you achieve your dreams? Would you still be depressed? Would you still have anxiety? Would you still be self-conscious about your body? All of these things are achievable. Once you figure out what you want, you can begin to lay out a path to get there.

Here are some questions to help you look honestly at your life. Answer these questions truthfully, for lying to yourself will only negatively affect and prolong your journey towards success. If you are completely honest with yourself, you are already heading in the right direction.

Are you doing what you truly want to do?

Do you have the career of your choosing?

Family life of your dreams?

Do you wake up every day excited and happy to start the day?

Are you living your ideal life? If not, what would you change?

Do you worry about money?

Do you trust your partner?

Do you downplay your achievements?

What are you scared of?

What lights you up?

Do you keep your word?

Have you fulfilled the promises that you made to yourself? Have you fulfilled the new year's resolutions that you make every year but give up on by the first week in February? How about the nights when you promise that you will get up early but when morning comes, you attack the snooze button? Make sure that you fulfill the promises that you make to yourself. You deserve it to fulfill your own promises most of all.

Will you break the rules for something or someone you care about? Is there a person in your life who will help push you even when you can't push yourself? When you use up all the fuel in your tank, who makes sure you keep moving forward? If not for yourself, will you change your life for someone else? Will you work hard today so your children can have a better future?

Is there anything you can't let go of, but know you should? Maybe there's an addiction you want to drop but just keep pushing it off. Maybe there's a toxic person in your life that you know you should get rid of. Maybe you can't let go of the fact that you had a rough childhood and that trauma is still eating away at you because you keep pushing the pain away instead of facing it.

Do you remember anyone you hated 10 years ago? Does it matter now? Maybe you're letting this person still live inside of your head. Are you still letting the words or actions of another person dictate and manage how you live your day-to-day life?

If you'd die now, would you have any regrets? Maybe it's that dream in the back of your mind that you have always wanted to accomplish. Maybe it's that business idea you have always wanted to act on but have been too scared of what your peers will say to do anything. If today was your last, then would you be happy with the results of your life? The scary thing is that we never know when our last day will come. Don't wait until then to decide you should have taken action. People usually only regret the things that they didn't do.

What's the difference between you and most other people? If you're reading this book, chances are you're searching for change. You probably don't want to be average like everyone else. What distinguishes you from other people? Is there something that you know you can do really well? Maybe a talent or a special skill, or maybe that immaculate passion you have inside of you. I know that you're special, and I know that something separates you from the crowd. What is it?

If today were the end of the world, what would you do? Do you have any loose ends that you want to tie up? Maybe you left someone on bad terms and want to apologize so you can move on. Would you cry because the world is over and there is so much you didn't do? Or will you smile and be happy because you lived your life to the fullest and never backed down from a challenge?

Take all of these things into account. Once you have a clear picture of how you want your life to change and what you want to fix. It is time for you to stop at nothing to achieve this dream life. Don't let anything or anyone get in the way of your happiness. They have no right to take that away from you.

In my dream life, I have freedom. I can travel across the world and take on new experiences. I have achieved financial success through my multiple businesses. I am surrounded by friends and family who love me. I have the time to be healthy and care for my body and mind. I have fun while making money. I get to live somewhere that inspires me. I am well connected. I follow my word and never let myself down. I am proud and confident in the life I have created. I do my best to be a good husband and father, and I'm creating a family legacy that will last longer than I will. That's what my dream life looks like. I have everything written down in more detail, but that's the basic idea of what I strive for.

Maybe you don't know what your passion is yet. Maybe instead of looking forward, you need to look back for the answers. Think back to your childhood days. Your early years in life. Every kid has a wild and crazy dream that they want to accomplish. We have such big dreams as a kid, and as we grow older, we tell ourselves that we cannot accomplish them for whatever reason. I need something that is realistic. I want a stable job and a stable income. I don't have what it takes. I missed my chance. Do these excuses sound familiar to you?

As we grow older, we tell ourselves these things are impossible for whatever reason. We give up on our childhood dreams for many reasons that we tell ourselves are justified. Did you give up on your childhood dream? Is there still an old dream in you? Maybe you don't know what your passion is. When you look back on life, you look at the person you were before the excuses hit. You will be able to discover that passion without all of the distractions and excuses. The innocence of childhood can be the spawn of great passion.

You Have Potential

This is very sad but, unfortunately, very true. Many of us count ourselves out before the race even begins. We forfeit the fight before we even step in the ring. We never even realize the potential we have. People go through their entire life without realizing they have the ability to do amazing things. I'm talking about truly amazing things. We have this idea in our heads that living our dreams is only for those who are "special." Only those who are rich or pretty or athletic can live their dreams. Success is for other people, right? Not me. WRONG!

Every one of us has limitless potential. But, to tap into it, you first must realize it is there. Most people immediately write themselves off as average or sub-par for any reason they can. Social media has us believing that everyone else is perfect. Everyone is rich, hot, and successful except for me. The truth is, everyone puts their best foot forward on Instagram. Also, don't believe everything that you see. You only see the tip of the iceberg on social media. You are only seeing what people choose for you to see. You see the trophy, but not the countless hours behind the scenes working on getting there.

Success is for everyone who earns it. That's it. It really is that simple. But first, you must realize your potential. Everyone CAN live their dream life and achieve success. Not everyone WILL, but everyone can. They don't believe they can do it, or no one has ever told them they can. Every single person on planet earth can change the world. It's all inside of you; if you can harness that potential, you will be unstoppable.

For reference, here is a list of people who grew up from nothing and became billionaires. These are true rags-to-riches stories.

Kenny Troutt, the founder of Excel Communications

Howard Schultz of Starbucks

Ken Langone, one of the founders of Home Depot

Oprah Winfrey became the first African American TV correspondent in Nashville

Shahid Khan of Flex-N-Gate

Kirk Kerkorian, the mega-resort owner

John Paul DeJoria, the man behind a hair-care empire and Patron Tequila

Do Won Chang, the founder of Forever 21

Ralph Lauren, the fashion designer

Francois Pinault, the luxury goods mogul

Leonardo Del Vecchio, the sun glass manufacture for Ray-bands and Oakley

George Soros, Legendary trader Li Ka-shing of Cheung Kong Industries manufacturing and real-estate investing

There are many other rags-to-riches stories worldwide, but this is just a very small list of people who defied the odds, went against what society told them, and became billionaires regardless of the poor situations or home life which they were born into.

Blame

It's quite common for us to blame our faults on everyone and everything. I catch myself doing it too. You begin to have control over your situation once you take total responsibility. Sometimes the situation that you are in is completely not your fault. Maybe someone took advantage of you, lied to you, or screwed you over. That sucks. We cannot control what people do to us, but we can control how we respond to the things they do. You are the only one who can create success for yourself, but you are also the only one who can guarantee a life of misery. The choice is 100% yours.

I spent five years of my life living in Grand Rapids, MI. During my time there, I learned a lot about myself and the person I wanted to become. One early Sunday morning, a hit-and-run driver totaled my car. My car was parked right in front of my house, minding its business. This driver, whom I presume to be a drunk driver, smashed their SUV into my little Ford Focus and completely destroyed it. Then, they drove off, never to be seen again.

I had very basic insurance coverage on my car at the time (Michigan car insurance is notoriously expensive), so I just had minimal coverage on the car. Basically, because I didn't know the person's personal information, I wasn't getting any insurance money for my car. Someone destroyed my car, ran off, and I was out of a car. After the incident, I contacted the police and tried to get something done, but they never found the criminal. I was out of a car, money, and put in a really bad spot. This was not my fault at all. Someone took advantage of me for their own gain.

This sucked. I was upset and angry for a while, but those feelings aren't productive. I did not pick myself up by blaming whoever wronged me. I had to suck it up, take what I could from the situation, learn what I could, and move on. Blaming other people for anything will never bring you closer to your goals.

Although it may make you feel better to blame other people for your lack of success. We cannot control each other's actions, but we can control how we respond to them. We can choose to let these things bother us, choose to get caught up in them, and we can choose to let roadblocks bring us to the point of failure. But pushing the blame on other people and situations will never bring a positive outcome to your life. Your best bet in a bad situation like this is to learn from it, do the best you can to better your situation, make sure that it doesn't arise again, and keep moving forward.

Be Obsessed

People are going to think that you are weird. People might look at you funny or say mean things because you are not doing what is "normal" to them. People will be baffled that you decide to go to the gym on Friday night instead of going to the bar. Successful people are weirdos. They are so obsessed with their specific field of study that others can't even fathom it. In order to get the goal, you will need to do some things others see as odd. After all, they call it the 1% for a reason. You need to be odd to be number one. You need to be obsessed.

My only friends are interested in the same three things that I am. That's business, cars, and fitness. Those are the only three things I ever talk about. That's just who I am. Do you have a hobby that you obsess over? Maybe a passion that no one else seems to care about?

Please don't let that passion go. It's ok to be obsessed. It's a good thing! Those who are obsessed with their goals are the ones who achieve them.

Step Out of Your Comfort Zone

In order to reach your dream life, you will need to do things you have never done before. In order to get the things you do not currently have, you must do more than you are currently doing. You will need to step out of your comfort zone. Throughout this journey, you will be uncomfortable, and it will be scary. But THAT IS THE POINT! Being uncomfortable is a GOOD thing. That means you are doing new things and learning.

You are not succeeding at your highest potential if you are within your comfort zone. Your success will start to show when you push the boundaries you have falsely set up for yourself. Your limits are not real. They have only been created in your mind. If you went through life doing the same things that you felt comfortable with, you could expect nothing less than the results would you have already been receiving.

Generally, people don't like change. That's normal. Change makes us feel weird and unusual. We don't want to be surrounded by unusual people, places, and actions. This is a feeling that you will need to battle with using all of your strength. The place you are currently at is located inside your comfort zone, but your dream life is outside of your comfort zone. Many great achievements are stuck behind the fear of rejection, stage fright, or failure. You cannot go around these feelings. You must go through them straight on. The more you step out of your comfort zone, the easier it becomes.

Why should I step out of my comfort zone? I like it here. The reason why you should step out is that you need to step out of your comfort zone in order to reach your fullest potential and blossom into your true self. Life begins outside of your comfort zone.

The world is changing now more than ever and at a faster pace than ever. This is true across the board but more relevant in some areas than others. If you are stuck in your comfort zone, then you will not be able to change with the times and adapt to our ever-changing world. Those who do not evolve get left behind.

So how exactly do you get out of your comfort zone? You simply do the thing which you fear. Don't make it more complicated than it needs to be. One of the most common fears is public speaking. I had this at one point too. However, by consistently practicing public speaking, I got over it. But I needed to get out of my comfort zone in order to destroy this fear.

For about eight years of my life, I was in theater and on-screen acting. I was in many live performances and some commercials, and extremely small movie rolls. This really helped me to become a better public speaker and gain confidence that was only found outside of my comfort zone. Now, this experience has helped me tremendously. I have been able to use my skills to start a YouTube channel. I have learned how to speak fluently on camera and clearly articulate my points. None of this would have been possible without stepping out of my comfort zone.

YOUR CURRENT SITUATION

Don't Stress What You Can't Change

You are not in control of what happens to you; you are in control of what you do about it. So many people get caught up in their surroundings and environment that they don't actually take time to improve their lives and push forward. Some of the go-to excuses that this person will use include sayings like; oh, they just got lucky, oh, they have rich parents, oh, it just comes easy to them. While there are so many things that we can't change, such as our race, the family that we were born into, or how some people may treat us, you can't get caught up in all this white noise. Take control of the parts of your life that you CAN change and forget about the ones you can't. You can't change your parents, the financial situation you were born into, or your genetics. However, you can sure use this information to fuel you and inspire you to create a better life for yourself.

We are not the product of the things that happen to us; we are only the product of how we respond. There will be things in our life that happen to us that we cannot change. We can only change the way that we react to those events. You will never grow if you continue to dwell negatively on the event. I get it. Trust me, I really do get it. Life is hard. Sometimes things happen to us that we don't deserve. Life isn't fair, and it sucks going through the hard times. But, there comes a time when we need to move on and go on and push forward. Deal with the situation and take responsibility for fixing it. We cannot continue wasting valuable time, energy, and headspace on the things we truly can not change.

For example, let's say that someone does you wrong. One of your best friends stabs you in the back. It may hurt that they did you wrong, and it may make you upset. It's not your fault that someone else hurt you. But that doesn't mean you aren't responsible for your own happiness. Are you going to spend the rest of your happiness worrying about how they did you wrong? Or are you going to take responsibility for your own life and find a way to be happy again?

Here's a new situation, if you have $86,400 in your bank account and someone steals $10 from you. Would it make sense to spend $86,390 to get your $10 back? NO! You have 86,400 seconds in the day. Don't spend your whole day worrying about something that took ten seconds of your time. Don't let the things in life that you can't change hold you back from succeeding in the things you can change. If the event is truly out of your control, don't dwell on the situation, but if it is within your control to change the situation, why are you sitting around crying and complaining about it? Go out and be the change that you want to see in your life. No one is going to do it for you.

The Way Others Treat You

This one is huge. Probably one of the biggest roadblocks that people face in taking their life to the next level. I'm going to start off with other peoples' opinions of you because this seems to be the biggest. As unfortunate as it is, people have gone to great lengths, such as suicide, because of what other people say about them. So many people are scared to put themselves first and put themselves out there. They are too scared to push because they don't know how other people react. They are afraid of what other people might say about them.

Plain and simple, you can't be a people pleaser. You can not and will not ever please everyone. If you spend your life doing what other people want you to do, you will miss out on what you want to do. Regardless of whatever you do, good or bad, right or wrong, people will judge you. So seriously, just do whatever the heck makes you happy. Because at the end of the day, if you're happy, that's all that matters.

There will always be people who think that your idea is stupid. People who think it's never going to work and don't believe in you. Let me get you in on a little secret; you're going to see those people later on in life. They will be contacting you asking you for a job, or telling others how they knew you. No matter who says these things to you and who doesn't believe in you, it is imperative that you push through. Your future self will thank you for this.

Unfortunately, sometimes this negativity comes from the people closest to us. But you cannot let that hold you back. Don't hold back or hide your potential because you are scared of what other people will say. Someone more successful than you will never talk down to you. Hate usually comes from jealousy, envy, or those below you. I know this is easier said than done but it's a skill you must learn to master. Once you stop caring is when you start living.

I Don't Care Who You Are

In order to get control of your life, you must accept responsibility for your actions and accept the current situation you're in. You're not broke because of him or her or anybody. No one else is responsible for taking care of your body. Some people are born in awful circumstances. The situation you were born into is not your fault. There are probably lots of things in your life that aren't your fault. But that doesn't mean they are not your responsibility to fix. At a certain point, you have to accept the reality of your situation. Realize that nothing in your current situation is going to truly change unless you change. Maybe people did you wrong, but you have full control of how you respond to what they do.

We cannot control outside situations, but we can control how we react to those situations, which makes all the difference. Maybe you were born with diabetes or a bad medical condition that causes you to gain unhealthy weight. You can blame the stars and the sky for being out of shape. However, nothing about the situation is going to change unless you go to the gym, diet, and take full control of the situation. That is the only way you will achieve the desired outcome.

Bottom line, anyone can do it. There's no sugar-coated version where I tell you everything will be okay, and success will just fall into your lap. Everyone can, but not everyone will. Once you realize your potential, that is when the magic starts to happen, and things get kicked into high gear. I don't care who you are, but you can do amazing things. No matter your background, race, or financial status, you can do amazing things and live your dreams. Don't cut yourself short, and don't let anyone tell you otherwise, no matter who they are.

Everyone Has Resources

There is an abundance of resources out there. You don't need money to have access to information. You can learn literally how to do anything on the internet by going through forums, watching YouTube videos, listening to podcasts, etc. Regardless of your social status or wealth, you can be educated on a limitless number of topics. If someone is in search of how to better their life, how to become a better business man, or how to work on a car, the knowledge is at your fingertips. Knowledge really is power, and knowledge is also money. If you get hired for a job, chances are that they hire you because you possess a skill of some sort. You would be surprised how many problems the internet can find answers to. Even the physical library is an amazing resource that the general public does not use.

There's got to be someone else who has done something similar to what you want to do. Right? You can't be the first person in the world who wants to start their own business or lose weight. Want to make it into the NFL? Look at current star athletes and their stories. What type of challenges did they overcome, and how did they succeed? You don't necessarily have to be all alone in this. There are many people out there who have told their stories of how they succeeded and give a detailed description of how they got there. This information is usually free, just Google it or look it up on YouTube.

Let's go through a fictional example of a young boy who is stuck in life. This young man utilizes the knowledge at his public library. Let's say that this 18-year-old was born into an awful family situation. His parents abandoned him, so he was forced to get a place for his own and fend for himself. This boy never completed high school, and he has no college education, but he has always wanted to start his own business. Unfortunately, he has no idea how. He went to the local library because he had no computer and couldn't afford one. He spent days researching business and learning as much as he could. He wanted to find a business that he could start with little capital because he didn't have much to invest, and he had to pay rent and food.

He concluded, after his research, that he wanted to start a landscaping company. To start off, he wanted to cut lawns. He did more research and found the right tools he would need to start off and learned how to cut lawns properly. After some practice, he learned how to present himself professionally. This young boy decides he needs to buy a truck and a lawnmower just to start. Once he brings in money, he wants to buy more lawn equipment. He finds out that his total investment will need to be around $5000. But there's a problem; he only has $2000 to spend.

This boy decides to get a job to save enough money to start his landscaping company. He gets a job working 50 hours a week at a landscaping company making $15 an hour. While working at the landscaping company, he is able to practice his skills and become better. He also asks as many questions as he can because he wants to learn from his boss about how to properly run a landscaping company. He can use his boss as another resource. After working for a while, he is starting to get close to his savings goal, and he decides to go back to the library and use their resources to print up some fliers so that he can pass them out and start collecting clients for his new landscaping company.

Finally, he has enough money to buy the equipment he needs and he could collect a few clients to start off with. Now that he is in business, he cuts his "day job" hours in half. He spends half of his time working at his job and the other half on his business. This includes cutting lawns and collecting new clients. Now, it's time to grow. He goes back to the library and sets up a few social media accounts for his company. He uses these to display his work, get word out about his company, and try to gain new clients. After a while, it starts to work. He is bringing in new clients and has enough to quit his day job and run the business full-time. Also, he decided to buy some other lawn care equipment like a leaf blower and a weedwhacker to make his lawns look nicer.

Using his resources, he finds some kids that need a job. He decides to hire one for his team. This gives him more time to research business and bring in more clients. He repeats this cycle, learning and growing out of poverty while setting his business up properly. He used the resources he had to learn a skill and then apply it.

I'm not sure what your goal is. But, I am sure there are actionable steps out there that you can use to succeed. I have tried my best to put many of them in this book. However, this book will not give you field specifics. All of the information you need to succeed is already at your fingertips. All you need to do is go get it. Think about your own life and the resources you might have. Maybe you don't have money, but you might have time. Maybe your weekends are open, and you can use that time to work on your goal. Maybe you live in a specific part of the world close to a certain industry. For me, I live in Detroit, Michigan. So, there are lots of opportunities in the automotive world for me. I know you have some resources you can use. What are they.

STRUCTURE

Work Hard, Using Your Time

Time is the greatest equalizer of all. Some people have more money than others from birth. Some people have certain physical advantages over others or maybe certain talents. But every single person on this earth has 24 hours in a day. No more, no less. I don't care who you are or how much money you have. We all have the exact same amount of time in the day. The difference between those who succeed and those who fail is how we choose to use this time. Top tier athletes are so successful because they are up at 4 AM training while most people are still sleeping. You have the potential to create for yourself a daily routine that, once repeated, will bring you straight to your goals.

It's crazy, if you set a goal and then set a daily routine with specific steps to get to that goal. By some stroke of magic, you somehow land pretty damn close to that goal. You can look at a person's daily routine and determine where they will be in 5, 10, or 20 years.

Do you have good or bad habits right now? Habits can sometimes be very hard to break. Even from down to the physical level, such as addiction. But the breaking of current habits and the formation of new habits is essential to success. Once you make it a habit to work towards your goals and improve your life every day, these repeated actions or new habits will lead you toward a life of success.

New habits become easier once you get going. For example, if one of your new habits is to wake up early, the more you start waking up early, the easier it gets. Soon, it will become normal for you to wake up early, thus leading to a more productive day. Once working on your dream becomes a habit, then you'll make continuous ground toward your goals.

Scheduling

Now OK, so you've realized that it's a great idea to change your life. Congratulations! But wow, that's a big bill, so you may think there's so much to do. Where do I even start? What do I do, and how do I do it? Well, one of the best ways you can organize yourself is through specific scheduling. Basically, what I mean is to schedule yourself a certain time every day that you complete a task. For example, if one of your goals is to hit the gym every day, hit the gym at the same time every single day. This will also help you to make progress and become more efficient. Develop a habit, and once you continually do something, it will become routine.

You might not have a lot of available time. Right now, I have a full-time job, part-time job, run a small business YouTube channel, hit the gym seven days a week, and I'm writing this book and doing all the normal life tasks. So trust me, I get it. I have used scheduling to help me get the absolute most out of my day. My ideal weekday schedule looks like this. Wake up around 4:30 am, workout from 5-6, work from 7-3ish, then I fill the rest of the day with either my business or this book. Then, on weekends I will sometimes work my part-time job.

Waking up early is the biggest scheduling hack I've found, and it has worked well for me. Having a relative time of day that I do specific things also helps me to do them better. I can do them faster and stay on schedule. I also like to keep a regular checklist of random things I need to get done to help me stay on task. Does every day look like this? No. Sometimes I get lazy and sleep in, sometimes, I need to travel for work, or sometimes other things just need my attention.

We all have the same amount of time. No one on this earth gets more time in the day than someone else. How you schedule your time will determine how much success you will achieve. Show me your schedule, and I'll show you your future.

Habit Forming

Habits are something that we do every day. They are actions imbedded deep into your routine that just come naturally. You don't even have to think about them. Habits can be good or bad, but regardless, they shape the person you are becoming.

Human beings don't like change. If you implement good habits into your routine, then it will start to feel uncomfortable to stray from these good habits. It also makes it easier to succeed when these good things come naturally. That is how you create a good habit and then stick to it. Getting started is absolutely the hardest part, but once you pass a certain point, this new habit becomes normal, and it's much easier to do things you're used to doing.

I have some good habits that I don't even think about. They just come naturally. Like drinking water. Once I started drinking water solely, I don't even like anything else. My body craves water over soda or other sugary drinks. It's natural now.

Scientific study show that it takes 66 days for a new habit to become automatic. Meaning that fully mind and body, you are accustomed to doing this activity. It is completely routine at 66 days. It will take some dedication, but it starts to get easier after the first few days. I would also recommend completing these habits at the same time every day. Making them part of your routine makes them easier. You will get to a point where you can't live without these healthy habits.

Let's use the example of our friend Joey who wants to lose weight. Joey decides that he wants to go to the gym at 5:30 PM after work every day and at 5:30 PM on weekends after he drops his kids off at baseball practice. Joe needs to do this for 66 days until it becomes normal, and he won't have to think about it anymore. Now, for Joey to succeed in making this habit routine, he needs to practice consistency as much as possible. He will need it on the days he feels like giving up. Joey should go to the gym at the same time, if possible, every day. Whether Joey wants to do strength training, cardio, or even just stretching and walking on the treadmill. Completing the action of going to the gym is important for forming a healthy habit.

At first, it may seem like this is a lot of work, and 66 days is a long time before a habit becomes fully automated. But it's really not that complicated. Over time, it will just become a thing you do, part of your normal life. Think of all the other things you do by habit most days and you don't even recognize them. Maybe drive your kids to school every day, or maybe you're younger, and you go to class yourself every day. They can be as simple as maybe you eat dinner at the same time every day or go to church every Sunday or whatever. So many people have habits and structures to their life, and they don't even realize it. If you can form a simple habit like eating at the same time every day, you can form a habit like going to the gym, working on your business, or developing your skill every day.

Sleep

Sleep is important. But it is also a waste of time. Was that confusing enough for you? I have a love-hate relationship with sleep. On the one hand, we all need sleep, which is an important part of our health. On the other hand, sleep can take up a large portion of our lives and tends to waste time. Like most things, a good balance of both is usually the way to go.

You only get 24 hours a day, and sleeping takes up a big chunk of that. Many people believe that they need 10 hours or 9 hours of sleep per night. I will admit that extra sleep is necessary for some extreme circumstances like professional athletics. However, for some of us, sleeping in is a guilty pleasure. I am part of that group. Unfortunately, sleeping in doesn't lead to success. Sleeping is a large part of our lives based on how much time it takes. If we can learn to manage it, then we can learn to manage 33% of our time.

Many largely successful people will tell you that six seven hours is a pretty good ballpark. It varies a little bit from person to person. That way, you still have a good chunk of the day left. Now you also want to make sure that you get enough sleep. If you're only getting three hours a night, you're not awake and functioning properly to complete your tasks efficiently and can't think properly. Another thing is health; your future isn't look bright if you get an extremely low amount of sleep every night for 20 years. Yes, being efficient is important, but you don't want to trade years of your life for hours in the day.

Oversleeping is also a problem. If you sleep too much, you will feel tired, groggy, and just not ready to perform properly. Basically, you have to find that sweet spot of enough healthy sleep but not too much to where you're damaging your body. If you can master your sleeping schedule, this will help tremendously to help you manage your daily life and schedule to use your time most effectively.

This is also one of those times when quality is more important than quantity. I am not a sleep expert, but here is what I have noticed. The quality of sleep that you get is more important than the number of hours you spend in bed. Once you hit the covers, ideally, you are exhausted and fulfilled from a long hard successful day. A good solid 6 hours of deep sleep usually does me better than 8 hours of tossing and turning.

Do not get me wrong. To succeed, there will be some days you get 4 hours of sleep or even no sleep. But it is good to develop some sleep rules for yourself. The goal: get as much sleep as you need to function at a high level and not a minute more.

Repetition

If you want to change, you will need to change your mindset. This includes changing the way that you talk to yourself. I coach myself through situations all day long. Repetition has helped me to change my mindset. What I mean by this is continuously telling yourself your goals and why you are doing this. Overtime, the things you say to yourself will become embedded into your self-conscience mind. Your good attitude will become second nature. Think of it like surrounding yourself with good people.

One of my favorite ways of doing this is setting my goals right above the bed where I sleep. On the ceiling, I see them every day right before I go to sleep and right after I wake up. It is there in the background all the time. Above my bed, I also keep a quote by Ryan Caraveo: "wishing every day for something doesn't count as dedication". So, that overtime if I'm struggling with a hard situation or feel lost and don't know what to do. My -consciousness kicks in and tells me to push forward and reminds me of my goal.

Many successful people talk to themselves a lot. A simple way of doing this can be just telling yourself I can do it or keep going. For example, if you're at the gym on your last set, you need to squeeze out those last wraps but can't seem to do it, keep telling yourself you can. Treat yourself with kindness, hold yourself up, and be your own best friend.

Waking up Early

One of the biggest hacks to living a successful life is waking up early. Discovering this was the best thing that ever happened to my schedule. I was never a morning person. I hated waking up early. That is, until I paired it with working out. My favorite way to start the day is waking up early and hitting the gym. It sets me up for success for the rest of the day. So much so that not doing my morning routine throws me off. If I miss my morning routine, I'm stressed, irritable, and just in a bad mood. Waking up early gives me a head start, and taking care of my body helps to relieve stress and make me better able to handle the day ahead.

Everyone's morning looks a little different depending on your career or lifestyle, but here's my ideal morning routine. I wake up at around 4:30 am, clean up, get dressed (with clothes set out the night before), and grab my pre-workout (also made the night before). Getting up early is hard, so I try to make it as easy as possible for myself the night before. I get to the gym around 5:00 am. Workout until about 6:00. Go home, shower, and get ready, then I get to work around 7:30 am.

As I said, this is my ideal morning. I don't always succeed, but this is the goal. I started off doing this routine in high school and have been in love with it ever since. Also, things change depending on my schedule. Maybe I'm traveling for work, or am I have deadlines to meet. I've learned to be flexible, but this is the general guideline I try and live my morning buy.

Obviously, your routine will be a little different than mine, depending on what your life looks like. But, I would seriously recommend combining waking up early with some sort of physical and mental activity. Something to get you ready for the day. Something to get your body moving and clear your mind for the day ahead.

You can use this to your advantage. Getting up early and getting after it will set you ahead of your competition. They may have some talent, but you don't need talent when you have hard work. You can craft your skill after hundreds or thousands of hours of dedicated time. You've got to get ahead of the game, and may not have the natural skill they have, but if they get up at nine and you get up at five. You've had hours of training before they even get out of bed. Creating a consistent schedule in which you wake up early repetitively will help you increase productivity and efficiency. Making sure that you get the most out of every day possible.

Waking up early is basically a hack to success. It's something that you can control completely, and it's something that will benefit you greatly. Think of how much better you will be at problem-solving if you come at your day with a clear mind. A large majority of successful people have some sort of morning routine. They follow this early morning rise with a strict morning routine, usually conducting some sort of physical or mental exercise to start the day.

I will say not to overdo it, though. At some point, you need to get the day started. Creating some massive 6-hour morning routine is probably not the best idea. By the time you wake up, get ready, workout, walk, journal, meditate, count your blessings, get a massage, and do your skincare, it's already past lunch. The morning routine does not replace the daily work you need to do. The morning routine puts you in a better place to complete that work.

FRIENDS

People Depend on You

You may not realize it, but your success does not affect just you. Think about your children or your future children. Think about your husband or wife. Think about all the people in the world that need your help. Who are you doing all of this for? Do you need to provide for someone? How will your family eat if you can't get up and find a job? How will you show your spouse that you love them if you don't put effort into the relationship? Are you going to sit by being lazy when there are people that depend on you? If something happened to a family member, and they could not support themselves, are you confident that you could take care of them?

You are an inspiration to others, even if you don't know it. You taking control of your life, subconsciously gives others permission to do the same. Someone will take inspiration from your story to make a change in their own life. Think of all the good you could do. All the people you could help. All the changes you could make. If you just gave it a shot.

Mentors and Influencers

We cannot choose the environment that we are born into. But we are 100% responsible for the environment we create around us. You can choose your friends, and place of work; you can pretty much change most things around you. You may have been born in a toxic or sub-par environment, but it's up to you to create a new one. In order to take your life to the next level, you need to surround yourself with people who are also doing the same thing. Star athletes hang out with other star athletes just like millionaires hang out with other millionaires. You become who you surround yourself with, and if you surround yourself with bad people, chances are you will start doing bad things as well. If nine of your friends are drug addicts, who do you think the tenth will be? These people will help you get to the top, and they can act as mentors and as a good influence. Their positive vibes, work ethic, and inspiration will rub off on you.

The people who you surround yourself with have a great impact on your life. But how do I surround myself with the people I admire? Some of the people I look up to are not exactly easy to get ahold of. They are billionaires and high-level business people. It's tough to sit down and get advice from people like Warren Buffett. Actually, Warren Buffett auctions off a dinner with him for charity every year. The last dinner sold for $19 Million. I don't know about you guys, but I don't exactly have that kind of cash lying around.

I may not be able to be friends with some of the most successful people in the world. But I can still bring their knowledge into my life. I can read a book that they wrote, listen to their podcast, and learn how they go about challenging situations. I can bring these people into my life by consuming their written content, videos, or music. The influences you surround yourself with affect the way you think. You may not always be able to personally chat with these people, but there will be some successful person out there online answering your questions. Regardless of your field of interest.

On the contrary, surrounding yourself with alcoholics, drug users, or bad influences will do you more harm than good. They will not only restrict you from receiving good influence but also pull you back. You don't want to put in all this work to have other people try only to take it away from you. I always ask myself this question, do I want to be going where they are going? In five years, would I trade places with them?

Don't be an asshole about it. But to change your environment, you need to cut out the people who are not right for you. I'm not saying that these are BAD people, but they just aren't going in the same direction as you are. They probably aren't actively trying to drag you down or make you a bad person. They may have been your friend since second grade, but they sit around broke all day playing video games, smoking weed, and drinking. Let's be real; that's not much of a winner, friend. You should always encourage those around you to come along for the journey. Try your best to lift them up. But the choice is theirs at the end of the day if they want to change their life.

This next one is a practice that has made my life a lot easier. It has helped me make decisions much easier and faster. Life is much easier when you trust the experts in their field. Here is what I mean by this. I would consider myself an expert on a few select topics. Everything else I don't know much about. So, if I need help in another field, I ask the expert in that field.

A few months ago, I wanted to start a new project on my car. I was going to install a new cam in my corvette, do all the work myself, and film the whole process on my YouTube Channel. I run a YouTube channel where I film myself building cars, racing, and other cool things. I'll talk more about that later but if you want to check it out, look up Cayleb Pletos on YouTube. Anyways, if you don't know what a cam is, it helps you bring in more air and fuel, allowing the car to go faster. It also sounds REALLY COOL.

This was a much bigger project than I had ever taken on, so I needed help figuring out what to do. One of the toughest things when building a car is figuring out what parts you need. I called up the company I wanted to purchase all of my parts from and spoke to one of their technical guys. I basically said here's what I want to do. I don't want to spend a whole lot of money, but what are the parts I absolutely need to make this happen? Also, are there any supporting mods that you highly recommend? I was looking for how to get the best value out of the parts I was purchasing.

Their team pointed me in the right direction. They showed me all my options, helped me pick out the parts that fit my needs, and answered my questions. They also helped me stay within my budget. That 20-minute conversation probably saved me 8 hours of research. Even after my own research, I would still have no idea if the parts I chose were correct. Plus, I really didn't want to mess this up and ruin my car. That would be a really expensive fix.

I will admit that this tactic won't always work. I would be careful who you ask. Hearing the words "what do you recommend" is a salesman's dream come true. Some people are out to make money off you, and some are actually here to help. However, this tactic has helped save me lots of time and headache. Trust the experts around you.

Surrounding Yourself with Good People

Outside influences can be strong, but you should be the only one who chooses how to live your life. Do what you want, not what society wants or not what your friends want, and not what your parents want. Others will try to fit you into their idea of what life should be like. You may go to high school, where they push every student to go to college and get a four-year degree. But, if that is truly not what you want to do and you want to take up a trade instead, don't be sucked into society's standard of what your life should look like. Do what makes you happy, not the people around you, because they're not living your life; you are.

Take a step back and ask yourself what I want for myself regardless of what other people think and how crazy or ridiculous they may deem me for having this dream. What do I truly want out of life? That's the question that you have to answer for yourself. Once you make that up in your mind, just make a decision. I am going to do this, and this is how. What type of person do you want to be?

It is better to be the worst of the best than to be the best of the worst. If you are the least skilled in your peer group and surrounded by great teachers and examples, you will learn from them. If you are the best of the worst, you will learn nothing because everyone around you has nothing to teach you. Surround yourself with people that you can learn from.

There comes a time after analyzing the people who you spend the most time around, that we realize we've got a few people who we really shouldn't be associating with. If I were to ask you, where do you see your friends going in five years or ten years? The answer to that question is probably not far off from where you're headed. If you look at someone else and say, "I don't think there going anywhere in their own journey", then chances are they shouldn't be part of your journey.

Your plans are greater, and you want to do more with your life. I'm not saying to banish your friends and family. You should always support those around you. But you should never hold yourself back or drag yourself down to someone else's level. I am also not saying you should be mean to others. Just recognize the paths you are both on. Are they the same? I'm just saying that you should love yourself enough and respect yourself enough to not let anyone hold you back from living your dream life.

Winners hang out with winners, and losers hang out with losers. People who are better aligned with your goals and dreams will push you farther than you can go alone. Remember, if you want to achieve this goal you need to stop at nothing, and there must be no limits to the type of things you will do in order to achieve this goal.

I'm not asking you to be a jerk to your friends; I'm just asking you to remove the toxic people in your life. I also encourage you to go out and meet new people in your line of work. Whatever your goal is, there have got to be people with the same interests. Find groups online, attend local classes, or meet people at events. Successful people are at these places. Healthy people are at the gym. Athletes are probably on the field. Rich people are probably running their businesses. You get the idea.

A good indicator of if somebody is a good fit for you. Ask yourself this question, now that you've gotten to them and now you've gotten closer to them has this person made a positive impact on you? Do they actually practice what they preach? Are they actually a good person? I'm not asking you to judge someone based on the things that they have; I'm asking you to judge them based on their character, integrity, and heart.

Who Cares What Others Think

Do you care what other people think of you? Being scared of judgment and ridicule by others is, unfortunately, a common setback for success. This holds back so many people from posting that video online or starting that business. Sometimes it's hard. Sometimes you can feel let down and attacked because you want more in life. Yea, I know it sounds crazy, right? Let's make fun of someone who wants to succeed. But it happens so often.

It's sad to say this, but the first people often to ridicule your goals or decisions are close relatives and family members. There may be many reasons why someone dares to ridicule your goals and dreams. Maybe they see you doing good and want to pull you down. Maybe they do it to make themselves feel better. Maybe they really just don't understand. Maybe all the above. If you want to be successful, you will need to deal with these comments. The sooner you brush them off, the sooner you focus on what really matters.

This being true, we are scared of ridicule and choose to avoid it at all costs, even if it means not pursuing our dreams. This is no way to live, basing your next life decision on what someone else will say or think about it. Let me say this: People will judge you no matter what you do, so just do whatever makes you happy. I don't think you understood that. Let me say it again for you. PEOPLE ARE GOING TO JUDGE YOU NO MATTER WHAT YOU DO, SO JUST DO WHATEVER MAKES YOU HAPPY!

Seriously, let's break this down. If you are poor, people will judge you. If you are rich, people will judge you. If you are attractive, people will judge you, but you will be judged if you are unattractive too. If you work hard, people will judge you, and if you don't work hard, people will also judge you. I could go on and on, but you get the point. Regardless of what you do, there is always someone to judge you for good or for bad. So, would you rather be judged and happy or be judged and devastated because you gave up a dream for someone you don't even like?

ACTION

Nothing Happens Unless You Work

Nothing happens unless you work. Everyone should work smart by planning their attack, analyzing their situation, and thinking over their options. However, action is the only thing that really pushes you forward. Yes, it is extremely important that you get yourself the proper knowledge you need and that you are continuously learning. But, throughout your life, action is the only thing that will directly bring results.

For example, if one of your goals is to achieve a certain level of personal fitness, then it is important that you learn about your body and the proper nutrients you need, what type of food you should be eating, and how much water you should drink. You should even research what exercises to do and how to do them properly. But at the end of the day, it doesn't matter how knowledgeable you are. If you don't put this knowledge to use, nothing gets done. Reading about losing weight will only get you so far. At a certain point, you actually need to do the activities.

There is this common notion that everyone successful got everything handed to them. We only usually see successful people after they are successful. We don't see the hours and hours they put in working before becoming successful. There is a false belief that success just falls on people randomly because they got lucky or had one good break. The fact of the matter of this is that it is simply not true. You won't achieve anything in the world unless you work for it.

The world doesn't owe you anything. The feeling that you can get something for nothing is a dangerous mindset and will surly lead you to a stagnant life. Desire is important, along with proper planning, but you will not get the desired results simply by wishing for it. Boots on the ground action is what actually changes lives. Action is the only thing that will directly bring results. You can think about success until you are blue in the face, but you will not get physically closer to your results until you act and put in the work.

Go!

Action is the only physical thing that brings you success. You can have all the motivation in the world, but nothing gets done if you don't act on it. The most successful people in this world are not the smartest. They are the ones who took action. Even if you are extremely knowledgeable, you will not see results until you take action. Sometimes we forget that action is the thing that gets us closer to our goals. Plain and simple, you will not make any physical progress without taking action.

I've noticed action is easiest when it's part of a habit. It helps me to continue progressing without having to think about it because it's just part of my day. Don't get caught up in analysis paralysis. There will never be a perfect time to start a business or start working out. The earlier you start, the better. The best time to plant a tree was 20 years ago; the second best time is today. You still need to do good work, but it is more important at first that you MOVE! Make ground, and you can worry about the little details later. Most people get caught up in the small details and never take action on their dreams. It is better to push for something than to get stuck analyzing everything so much that you never take action.

Action is also one of the best motivators. I love to sleep. But I also hate it. When my alarm goes off in the morning, I don't WANT to wake up. But I know that if I take action and get up, it will be so much easier to take the second action of the day then the third. It's a basic law of physics, an object in motion stays in motion unless acted upon by an outside force. If you are in motion. AKA if you are working on your goals daily. Then it is a lot easier to keep doing it. If you are staying still, you need to push to get started, and once you get the ball rolling, it's easier to keep it going.

Taking action is just like driving a car. You burn lots of gas accelerating (getting started) to get up to speed. But once you are up to speed, it only takes a small amount of gas to maintain your high speed. However, if you come to a complete stop (give up, quit, stop trying), it takes a lot more gas to get up to speed again. Be fuel efficient and take consistent action.

WORKING SMART

Time

Time is a limited resource; once we spend it, we will never get it back. This is why using your time wisely is so important. This helps you get the most out of the few hours of the day that you have to work with. Time will forever and always continue to tick by, so we must work hard now so we can enjoy the rest of our lives later. We cannot enjoy the fruits of our labor if we do not first plant the tree. If your friend works 40 hours a week and you work 100 hours a week, you can get done in 4 months what they can get done in a year. We all have the same amount of time in the day, but how we use our time separates the average people from the top performers.

It always makes me laugh when people say something like this: "I don't have time to work out". How can this make any sense? We all have the exact same time in the day. But this person doesn't prioritize their time so that they can workout. They always say they don't have time to go to the gym, but they sure seem to find time to binge Netflix every weekend. Please take note of how you are spending the hours in the day and if you are really using them to help build your dream life.

We can use little tricks like efficiency to squeeze as much out of the day as we can. This will help you jump ahead of the competition and excel faster than most on your path to success. In theory, it's a very simple concept. If you can rearrange your day to find two hours a day to work on your goal, you will achieve your goal in half the time as the person who only finds one hour a day to work on their goal.

We can also use the time to our advantage. Putting in hard time toward your goal will give you a tremendous advantage. I am not super talented, but I can show up earlier than the person who is. Hard work and putting in your time will beat talent in the long run.

Efficiency

I'll be the first want to say that hard work is very important, but it's not the only factor. Working smart is just as important. Being efficient ties into many different categories. My favorite, time and money. We have all heard this before, but these two really are correlated. Being efficient is all about how you use your time and money. We can learn how to work hard and smart and combine those with good time management skills. That way, we are not wasting effort.

We all have the same amount of time. We all get 24 hours in a day. The richest man in the world and the poorest both have the same 24 hours. How we budget, schedule, and use our 24 hours brings us efficiency. Some tasks are worth our time, and some are not. It is up to us to understand which tasks are worth our time. I prefer to focus on the most important tasks, delegate the smaller tasks, and forget about the small things that bring no value to my life.

So how does money tie into this? Well, your time has value. Maybe you are a self-employed business owner, or your employer pays you on some sort of an hourly basis. Even if you are salary, you can get a pretty good idea of your hourly rate. For example, $100,000 per year boils down to $50 per hour. This assumes the standard 40-hour work week with two weeks of vacation. I strongly recommend you find out what your hour hourly rate is. That way, you can have a relative understanding of which tasks are worth your time and which ones are not.

Let me throw you through a hypothetical situation. At your home, you cut your own grass and tend to the lawn every week. This takes you two hours. At your job, you make $50 an hour. So, to cut your own lawn, costs you $100 of time. How much would it cost to hire out this service? It might cost less than you are paying. Let's say you find a company to do it for $50 a week. It would be more efficient for you to work one extra hour that week at your job than to cut your own grass. Plus, the professionals probably have much better equipment and can do a better job.

What if you only make $20 an hour? Then it is worth your time to cut your own grass. This way, you would save money in the long run.

This scenario is pretty basic, but we can apply this lesson to all areas of our lives. If we want to get really efficient, we can specialize in one area that provides us with the most benefit, then outsource the rest.

Working hard is amazing, and you should always push yourself to the limits, but that's really only half the battle. All that hard work will go to waste if you are just spinning your wheels. From what I have gathered from my life experiences, there are three sections to efficiency. Working extremely hard, working smart, and continuous improvement. I encourage you to take a long look at how you spend your time. Is what you are doing really efficient? Are you getting the most out of your time spent? Are you using your finances to buy back your time?

Another great way to increase efficiency is to ensure you are using the proper tools to get the job done.

This may be the most up-to-date technology, faster internet speeds, or a better shovel. I'm not sure what your goal is, but I am sure you can use some tool to help you get there.

Ever since I was a young kid, I have always liked cars. I grew up in Detroit, the motor city. I enjoy working on my cars, and I have gotten pretty good at it over the years. I am no master mechanic, but I can do my fair share of work and fix common car problems. Whenever something brakes on one of my cars, I have some choices. Do I take it into the shop or fix it myself? How much time and money will this cost? Do I have the right tools to make the job go faster? I then make a decision. Getting your car fixed at the shop can be pretty expensive, so I usually do the task myself. I also have a decent size tool collection, so the job moves along faster than normal. I encourage you to find the most efficient solution next time you run into a problem.

Another area of efficiency is multitasking. Multitasking can be good or bad, depending on how you structure it. Personally, I like to keep it light. An example of good multitasking is combining learning with any simple repetitive task. You can listen to an audio book while you drive to work or cook dinner. This way, you learn while completing a relatively simple task. Multitasking can cause more harm than good in some situations, so you need to multitask wisely. It's probably not a good idea to read a book and watch a movie at the same time. Trying to pay attention to two things at once will only cause you to perform less on both. You are likely to read much slower, only retain a portion of the information you encounter, and miss important things from the movie.

Understanding the value of your time will bring you closer to success. It will help you to choose which tasks to do personally and which ones to pass off. We all have the same 24 hours, but being efficient can help us use them wisely.

YOUR BODY

Everyone Needs a Sanctuary

Everybody needs some sort of sanctuary. I mean that everyone needs a hobby, activity, or routine to return to. Something to relieve stress and keep them grounded. This activity acts as a reset button for the mind and body. It is usually some sort of ritual, physical activity, or mental activity. Examples of this include working out (my personal favorite), meditation, or just going for a walk. I use working out as a stress reliever, and it helps to keep me mentally sharp. If I have a bad day, I can go to the gym, blow off some steam, then revisit my challenges after I have cleared my mind.

I also like to practice mindfulness meditation when I find myself loosing focus. I did this a lot during my college years when writing for class. That gave me the time to breath, acknowledge the thoughts racing in my mind, and learn to let them pass. This helped me to stop chasing every individual thought that crossed my mind. That way, I could focus more on the task at hand.

Your sanctuary is a place where you can go to just be alone. No one is bugging you, and you get to focus on your task. In my case, lifting the weights in front of me. I think your sanctuary gets bonus points if it connects both the mind and the body somehow. Many successful people share a strict morning routine, mostly around a physical or spiritual activity such as prayer, exercise, meditation, or even journaling. I recommend doing this activity in the morning to clear your head before your day. This will help ensure you are strong and able to handle any challenge the day throws at you. If you are having a bad day, you can always count on that one thing to be there to help straighten you out.

Your Mind

Having a healthy mind and strong mental health is one of the most important topics in this book. We will dive deeper into mental health in later chapters, but for now, I think it's important you understand this. Your mind is the most powerful thing you own. You can think yourself into and out of any situation or mental state. Your mind will determine how you view and work through the different challenges in your life. Conquering your mind and yourself is one of the toughest battles. I struggle with it all the time. But it is also one of the most rewarding. Because once you learn to control that thing between your ears, there is no limit to what you can accomplish.

Your positive mindset will literally change how you live your life and look at your daily situations. Clearing your head of all the unnecessary baggage will help you focus on the important tasks. If there is no enemy within, the enemy outside can do us no harm.

When I feel weak or overweight, I go to the gym. If I want to get a stronger chest, I bench press. If I want to get stronger legs, I squat. If we want to get stronger muscles, we work them out. Our brain needs working out too. We can work out our minds by constantly making positive choices that align with our goals. We can train our minds and reprogram them, to help us consistently strive toward succeed. Continuously making good choices works out our minds.

Just like our muscles, we must feed our minds with good nutrients. The environment around us, influences, and people we hang around can all seep into our minds. For better or for worse. Our minds will grow and evolve if we surround ourselves with good mental nutrients. If we feed our minds junk like toxic relationships and garbage television, then our minds will begin to adopt the bad habits we see around us. Your mind can be either your greatest advantage or your biggest enemy. You decide.

Food

Let's face it. If you are reading this book, then you want to perform at a high level. You want to get the most out of life. You probably want to work very hard and efficiently to achieve your goals. In order to do all of these things, you need to eat healthily. You will operate so much better if you are fueled by healthy food.

Do you know what happens when you put race gas in a car? It goes faster! You can't be splurging on McDonald's and Burger King seven days a week and expect to perform to the best of your ability. Eating the right nutrients and ensuring your body gets what it needs will give you an extreme advantage. It is amazing what a difference proper nutrients, drinking water, and eating clean will make in your life.

Eating right may also be one of your goals. That's great! Maybe you have a goal like weight loss or working out. How you eat obviously effects these things. But it also changes the things we don't see. Healthy eating can change our mental state, how well we can focus, and our energy levels.

If you want your machine to run to the best of its abilities and be the fastest that it can be, then you put the right type of fuel into it. Your body is a race car. You can't expect to win the race with extremely poor-quality gasoline. Your engine will break down, you will put extreme ware on parts, and it will cost you money. Your body is the same way, if you expect to perform at the best of your abilities, then you need to be giving your body the proper fuel, and by this, I mean eating the proper nutrients and maintaining healthy habits. Above all else, it just makes you feel so much better.

CONSISTANT LEARNING

Don't Be Stubborn

The world is always changing. Your field of study is probably always changing too. Is your goal to start a business? The business field changes every day. In order to grow consistently, you need to be a student for life. In order to be a student, you need to be open-minded. You cannot learn if you believe you already know everything there is to know. If you are stuck and seeking advice, you cannot be stubborn. When you speak with a mentor or teacher, you will not be able to take in any information until you open your mind. If you want to learn the most, it is imperative that you come into the situation ready to learn. You cannot be stubborn if you wish to acquire the knowledge required to succeed.

Stubbornness can be detrimental to your success. Walking into a situation stubbornly will do you more harm than good. Let me explain, if I read a book on a topic related to my goal, and I read the book with the mindset of "I already know everything about this topic" then I will learn nothing. It will be advantageous to adopt the mindset "I am here to learn, teach me everything you know". This will allow you to learn much more and increase productive learning.

Mistakes

I make mistakes all the time. Like, seriously, every day. I have had to close a business, had failed relationships, and dug financial holes for myself. I've made mistakes I never thought I would come back from, but here I am today, still kicking. So, when I talk about mistakes, understand that I have a lot of experience.

The general attitude is that mistakes are bad and should never happen. The word mistake has such a negative connotation. Mistakes might hurt, but they are a necessary part of the process of success. If you fail, that is only a lesson. Some of the biggest life changes I have made have come from failure. The only way that a mistake can be a bad thing is if you don't learn from it. If you continuously do the same thing over and over and over again, expecting different results, you are insane. If you take a step back and analyze your mistake, you may change your actions and adjust yourself to be better on course toward your goals and dreams. That is a good thing. Learning from your mistakes and learning how to better yourself and innovate are beautiful skills.

Another thing about mistakes, you don't always need to learn from your own. There are plenty of articles and stories about how people failed and why they failed. You can learn from those so much. It is just as important to learn what not to do as it is to learn what to do. Learning from other peoples' mistakes is great, because you don't have to spend time making a mistake yourself. The road to success is anything but straight. It will throw you mistakes and failures, twists and turns, but as long as you learn to take a step back and adjust yourself accordingly, these mistakes will only be a minor setback in action and a large leap in knowledge.

Read

Reading is probably one of the best ways to learn and grow your knowledge base. You can pick up a book on anything. Unfortunately, only a small portion of the population reads and continues to grow their mind after they have graduated from school.

Many skills cannot be learned in a classroom or in school. The best sources of information are usually not in high school or college. Personally, I graduated high school and then college. I have a degree in accounting and finance. I would realistically say about 25% of my total knowledge has come from school of some sort. Most of my knowledge comes from outside learning like books or videos, people, or experiences. Also, books are

MUCH cheaper than school. Value per dollar, books beat college every time.

This brings us to the importance of surrounding yourself with knowledgeable people and people you look up to. I talked about this in other portions of this book that it is important to surround yourself with friends who have goals. Surround yourself with dedicated and ambitious people. Even if you try to stop it, your friends' habits will rub off on you, for better or for worse.

For most of the population, it is not realistic for us to sit down with celebrities or CEOs and ask them how they got there. But you can read a book they wrote, listen to a podcast they put out, or watch a video that they produced. You become who you surround yourself with, and if you surround yourself with books from successful people, their habits will rub off on you. You will learn from them and start to become successful too.

Why is knowledge so important? Because you don't know what you don't know. This is a concept that a lot of people, including myself, struggle with a lot. It's the concept that you don't know what you don't know. Once you determine the general topic you would like to learn about, you can pick up a book on the subject or get into some learning program. Once you get into this program you will be able to learn things that you never even knew existed. If you do not put yourself into that situation, you will never learn about the things that you do not know. These could be holding you back.

When I started my accountant job, I was so new that I didn't know anything. I understood the general idea from what I learned in school, but I was still a sponge in the workforce. The things that were common to my co-workers were not so common to me. I even had trouble understanding my colleagues because we had such a knowledge gap. However, I slowly became more and more knowledgeable about the business. I was exposed to all the successful people in my field and started to pick up on the things I didn't know.

Knowledge really is power. Once things start to click, it feels so good. You start to see things from a different perspective and understand things you never dreamed you would understand. You go from "I have no idea how this person accomplished this" to "this is actually simple, and I can easily outline the steps that this person took to success, and I can do it to". I swear knowledge can make you into a super human. Reading and learning sharpens your mind like a stone sharpens a samurai sword. After every book you read, your mind becomes sharper and a bit better until you get to the point that you can cut through tough problems with ease.

When I was younger, I read a lot more than I do now. I am busier than I was back then, but I still try and read about 10-15 books a year. I try to fit reading in when I travel or have some downtime. Reading books turned into a collection for me. I keep every book I read. I have two collections. One of the books I've read and one of the books I haven't read yet. Whenever I come across a book I think I might like, I'll usually buy it online, throw it into a pile, and get to it eventually. It's gotten to a point where I can pick a book from the collection that I think will help me in that moment. My book collection varies from finance to self-help to health to business. What do you want to read about?

Your mind is your greatest tool, your best asset. You can accomplish anything you dream of with the tool inside of you. The mind is the beginning of all great achievements. The human brain is powerful and becomes stronger after everything you learn. Utilizer this tool to its fullest potential.

Not Traditional Learning

You might have to stretch your imagination when learning about your dream life. You are going to need to think outside the box to get there. Many of the answers you are looking for will probably not be found in school. Not in a traditional learning environment. Plus, it's a lot cheaper if you look elsewhere. You can't usually take a class on how to live a healthier life and loose 30 pounds, for example. I'm not saying that school is useless, but I still wouldn't give it too much credit for my own accomplishments. You will need many more skills to become the best version of yourself, and the classroom will not give you everything you need.

Some of these topics I am referencing include managing your emotions, dealing with stress, being your own motivator, and independence from others. When I started my YouTube channel, I couldn't exactly learn that skill in college.

Learning from others is also a great source of information. Study the great people in your chosen field and see how they became successful. Study what types of problems they encountered and how they overcame these problems. Use other people's failures and mistakes to learn from. This will help prevent you from making the same mistake as others.

You need to do things a little differently. Perusing your dream life is not normal. You are the minority because you dare to ask for more out of life. You cannot be doing the same exact things as everyone else and expect to achieve a higher goal than them. If you read the same books as everyone else, you will receive the same knowledge as them. If you go to the same school as them, you will have the same resources that they did.

If you work as hard as everyone else, you will get where everyone else is going. Like everyone else, you need to consider your own decisions too. You cannot be doing the same thing every day and expecting a different result. That's insanity. If something doesn't work, try something else. If your teacher isn't teaching you well, then get a new teacher. Try different things and listen to the experts. Just don't get stuck doing the same thing over and over again because you will only get the same results over and over again.

Learn or Die

I'm not sure what your dream is. I don't know what you want out of life. I know I'm not the first person to tell you this, but the world can be a nasty place. It's sink or swim out here. Survival of the fittest is REAL. No one else cares about your problems. It's up to you and you alone to make your dreams a reality. Learn, read, try, grow, and experience as much as you can. Because your competition is coming and they are coming fast.

As technology progresses, humans are getting better and better. Athletes are getting stronger, scientists are getting smarter, and standards just keep going up. Just look at the job market. Jobs that only required a high school diploma now require a 4-year degree and 3 years of experience. Take a look at the field you are playing on. Who are you competing against?

As you probably know by now, I run a YouTube channel. My channel is competing against some of the smartest minds all over the world. I compete for viewers' attention against millions of channels in different time zones and countries. If I want to succeed, I need to be better than every YouTuber in my niche in the world.

Who do you need to be better than to succeed? What does your potential competition look like? Let's take a look at another example. Let's say you own a pizza restaurant. Growing up, I worked in a pizza restaurant for a few years, so pizza is always on my mind. Who are you competing against? The 3 other pizza places in your town? You are only really competing against those in your relative area. Your potential customers don't live 5 hours away. They probably live in your town. It's much easier to have the best business in town than the best business across the entire internet.

It is very important that you learn as much as you can about your dream. If somebody has a dream to become a CEO they should research everything and anything they can about CEOs. What are the world's top CEOs like? What kind of schools did they go to, and what did they study? How did they get there? How long did it take to become a CEO. Do all these people like being in their position, and how have they been able to help others since they have acquired this position? Is this something that you are willing to spend the rest of your life doing? Is this really what you want to do?

There is always someone younger than you, and if you let them, they will pass you up. Are you competing in the same market? In the same business? Or can everyone win together? The way to combat this is with consistent learning. Times will change, and technology will pass you up if you let it.

ROCK BOTTOM

Mental Health

This chapter is going to get pretty deep. I want to talk about feelings and experienced that I have been through with mental health. Your mental health is extremely important. More important than your physical health, but they tend to work together. I want to state that I am not a medical professional. If you think you need serious help, please get it. If you think you are at risk of harming yourself, please call someone. Your life is valuable, and you are loved. Things will get better even if it doesn't seem that way now. Throughout this chapter, I want to share my experiences with mental health and the remedies I use to stay healthy.

When I started writing this book, I was 18 years old. I thought I had it all figured out. I had lots of good habits, worked really hard, and had an amazing attitude toward life. I now sit here at 23 years old, reflecting on the past five years of my life. In the past five years of my life, I have gone through almost every emotion possible and some I thought I would never encounter. I failed, I lost, and my mental empire came crumbling down.

I was lost, and confused, and a lot of times, I couldn't understand how I was feeling. In the next few chapters of this book, I want to go over some of the things that I went through and how I overcame them. Also, I want to add a few lessons I learn along the way. While going through these challenges, I had to draw from my past experiences and from my prior knowledge. I had to learn to trust in the process and trust myself. I learned sometimes you have to follow what you know to be right and not how you feel.

At first, and a lot of the times while I was going through these things, it felt like this was the end of me.

Only after I came out on the other side did I realize that all of these things were necessary for me to go through to succeed. The point is I had to go THROUGH these things. I am so much stronger now that I have gone through all of these different challenges. These challenges will help you to get closer to mastering yourself. So, the next time these challenges come knocking, and believe me, they will, you will be so much more ready to handle them. You can't ignore your issues and expect them to go away.

Most of the time, I didn't even understand what was happening until I was deep in the middle of it. Different types of problems require different solutions. Each one of these different challenges had a different solution. Am I proud of the person I was at my lowest? Absolutely not, but you cannot judge a person based on their worst day. The solutions I used may not work for you and also do not replace professional help for mental issues. However, if you master your own mind, anything is possible.

Rock Bottom

For many of us, there will be an extremely dark time in our lives. A "rock bottom," if you will. You will most likely reach a point in your life where it seems like all hope is los. A time when you want to give up, turn your back on your dreams, the world, and hope. At this point, you have probably started destroying relationships in your life as well and pushing people away. All while digging yourself further into this hole. This can be a financial hole, physical, or mental health rut.

In these dark times, we must stick to what we know is right. It's very easy to make bad decisions under the influence of depression or anxiety. When you come to this rock bottom, you are faced with a choice. Give up and live with the pain of failure, or push through and suffer the pain of success. It is at this moment you have got to get up. Never never quit. You don't have to have all the answers, and the future might not look bright, but don't quit. Whatever you do, don't quit.

No matter how dark it may seem, you can truly come back from anything. You will change along the way and be molded by your experiences, but you will come out better on the other side. The human mind and body are capable of insane things. You can come back from anything. You can bounce back from bankruptcy or divorce or depression. Many people in this world have done it. Many of them are not as gifted as you. They're not as strong as you, they're not as smart as you, and they don't have the heart you do. We must look to these people as proof that it can be done. You don't have all the answers to get up and don't have to understand what you're doing to get up. None of us know what the future holds, but we work hard and trust that it will be better than the present because we will make it that way.

All you have to understand is that it's possible. You can live your dream life, and you can succeed in your goals. It's possible to achieve all of your wildest dreams. You just have to figure out how. Figuring out how will be very tough, but you will handle it like you have handled every other problem that has crossed your path. One step at a time. When we lose sight of our true purpose and get stuck in the daily challenges. When we get stuck at rock bottom, we must get up and keep getting up. Never never quit.

Depression

I went through a period of my life where I was depressed. I didn't fully understand what I was going through at the time, but it was some sort of depression. I spent days rotting in bed, slept almost all day, ate like shit, ignored my responsibilities, and distanced myself from everyone. It took me a while to get out of this, but this is how I did it.

I started off by focusing on the little things. If you can't do the little things right, you will never be able to do the big things right. I would focus on small tasks like doing the laundry, taking a shower, or making food. Doing that one small thing would give me the strength and momentum to do another and then another. Slowly, as I accomplished more, I started to dig myself out of this hole.

I was procrastinating like crazy at this time. I always told myself "I'll get up early tomorrow and do this," but I never did. I started to realize that action is what motivates us. Accomplishing tasks and doing things gives us the motivation to do more. When you are down and depressed, start small and create momentum through little actions. Don't wait for the perfect moment. You will never feel like getting up. The key is to do it anyways. Get up and do one small task. Just one small thing and see how you feel. Keep moving forward, use momentum, and never never quit.

Anxiety

Anxiety is a weird one. It's also one of the emotions that I hate the most. Unfortunately, it's one of the emotions I have struggled with the most. Mostly in the past few years. When I started dealing with anxiety and these anxious feelings, I did not understand them. For me, anxiety is very physical, and I feel it the most in my stomach. Anxiety never comes at me in a shocking panic attack way but in a slow, low, consistent stomach uneasiness. I absolutely hate it.

But, if you are going to be successful, you will have to manage stress. Big people have big problems, and when those problems come, you have to learn to be as cool as a cucumber. Like most of the experiences, I went through, they absolutely sucked going through them. However, I'm very thankful that I went through periods of anxiety. All of the tough challenges I went through have made me stronger.

There are lots of different things that can trigger anxiety in our lives. Maybe financial problems, health issues, or problems in our relationships. These issues can build up in our minds and come out as anxiety. The longer we avoid these issues and run away from them, the worse our anxiety gets. From my experience, my anxiety does not simply go away because I ignore it. I cannot ignore anxiety away. There is a reason for anxiety, and it is my job to figure out what that reason is and fix it. I like to fix these problems right away. If I get into an argument with someone, I like to settle it and make up as soon as I can. I don't like those feelings floating around for days and weeks. Ignoring your bank account will not change the fact that you don't have any money.

If you have anxiety, your body and mind tell you that you must face your problems. Even after acknowledging a problem, the anxiety starts to get better. The first step is marching straight towards our problems. Yes, it's uncomfortable. But this is what must be done if we want to cure our anxiety. As soon as you face that uncomfortable thing, the anxiety starts to fade. I promise that you cannot ignore your anxiety away. Trust me; I've tried. You must face your problems in order for them to go away.

Even though anxiety sucks, I don't want you to think that it's necessarily always a bad thing. Anxiety is natural. It is a natural part of being human. But, the natural aspect of anxiety can get messed up living in our modern world. Humans were built to live in the wild. Living in the wild, you face many real dangers. Anxiety was instilled in us to save our lives. Anxiety was meant to make us survive very dangerous threats. Long ago, if a human came face-to-face with a lion, they would get dosed with lots of anxiety and fear. This anxiety then forced them to run away and seek shelter. This was meant to save us. The issue is that in our modern society, there are not many circumstances where we come face-to-face with lions anymore.

So, we have this survival instinct built in us, trying to operate in a modern, relatively safe society. That is why we may get lots of anxiety over a small issue, and we might ask ourselves, "why does this feel like it's much more of a big deal than it is?" Your body's response is, "oh my God, there is real danger. We need to run," but in all reality, your friend Becca is just mad at you.

Anxiety can help you. It's your body's way of telling you that something is wrong. Something isn't sitting right with you, you feel in danger, or something is on your mind. Maybe you can use this to help clear up something that's holding you back from success.

In the modern world, everyone wants to pop pills to handle their mental health. At one point, my doctor asked if I wanted anxiety medication. I thought about it for a little but ended up declining. For me, anxiety isn't the problem. It's a symptom of the problem. Anxiety is what comes along when something else isn't sitting right. I will never feel any better trying to muffle the symptom. I really cure my anxiety by solving the actual problem that is causing the anxiety. Fight the problem not the symptom. For anyone struggling with this, know you are not alone. That may be scary, but you need to face it to start feeling better. Face your fears. You created them, and you can destroy them too.

Dedication

Dedication will take you places that motivation never will. Almost every day, we encounter things we don't want to do. We don't want to get out of bed, make dinner, or exercise. But giving into temporary satisfactions will absolutely destroy our self-esteem and long-term fulfillment. If we only worked on ourselves or hard on the days we felt like it, we would never get anything done. Being dedicated and proving to ourselves our dedication motivates us on its own. It's very easy to do the right thing when everything is going your way or when you're in the middle of that winning streak. But dedication is most important when we need it most, which is in our times of weakness.

Dedication is also a time game as well as a game of tricks. The human mind works very fast to try and convince us not to do things. Our mind wants to convince us to stay in bed or take the easy path. So, it's up to us to combat these feelings with swiftness. I like to trick my mind into doing what I know I need to do. For example, putting my alarm clock on the other side of the room so that I'm forced to get out of my bed to shut it off. Or, I might write a note the night before to my morning self, explaining the benefits of waking up early. The night before, waking up early sounds like a great idea, but my moment of weakness is when I'm tired and don't want to get up. That's when I need the extra motivation from past Cayleb.

Dedication doesn't always have to be challenging. Make it easy for yourself. Nobody likes to do hard things. One of the ways that success can be easier to achieve is by doing simple things to set yourself up for success. It is easier to do things we don't want to do if we make them easier. One of my favorite examples of this is in my morning routine. Getting up early sucks. When it's cold, and you're tired, and you didn't get enough sleep, it can be really hard to wake up at the crack of dawn. Ideally, I will start my day every day with the gym. It is my anchor that keeps me together. But sometimes I struggle with getting up and actually getting to the gym at 5 AM when I am supposed to.

Here is how I make getting up early and going to the gym easier for me. I love going to the gym, but getting there is the hard part for me in the morning. So, I reduce all the things that get in the way of me going to the gym. Getting dressed, cleaning up, picking up my clothes, finding my keys and headphones, grabbing a protein shake, and mixing up my pre-workout. These are all small things that take time, but they can be annoying, especially when you don't want to get out of bed.

So, I sent out my keys and headphones, picked out my clothes and set them out, and mixed up my pre-workout and picked my protein for after my lift. Everything is sitting out and ready to go as soon as I get up. It reduces the physical and mental blocks between me getting up and going to the gym. All I do is get up and brush my teeth, put in my contacts, and maybe brush my hair if it's a crazy day. I take care of all the other cleaning up things after I get home from the gym because there's no point in showering before I get all sweaty.

All I have to do is one task when I wake up. That is to simply get up so I can go to the gym. It is a lot easier to convince myself to simply get up as opposed to getting up and doing this list of chores. All I have to do is wake up and have a great workout. Recently, I have also done this more on the other side of my sleep routine. I do not set myself up for success if I stay up till 1 AM and set my alarm for 4 AM. No wonder I am tired in the morning and sleep through my alarm because I only gave myself three hours to sleep. If I get to bed at a reasonable time, then it's a lot easier to wake up at a reasonable time. Who would have thought right?

I use health a lot when explaining success because it's easy to understand, but let's go over a different example. Having healthy spending habits. Something I have also struggled with and still do from time to time.

Let's consider an example to help us control our spending habits. Only bring a certain amount of money to the function with you. Let me explain. Some people, like my grandma, absolutely love gambling. Personally, I'm not a huge fan. However, some people really struggle with controlling their money in a gambling setting. A common practice to help combat this is to only bring a certain amount of money in cash with you so that you are not tempted to spend anything else. You will not spend more money if you don't have it with you. It is very easy for us to fold in our moment of weakness, whatever that moment of weakness is, so we can do many things like this to make that decision easier.

Are there little things you can do in your day-to-day life to better set yourself up for success? We all have moments of weakness where we make the wrong decision, which makes us feel bad. We lose momentum to our goals, and it could potentially set us down a downward spiral. These things might not seem to make a big difference, but just give them a shot. One of my favorite quotes from a navy seal's speech says, "if you can't do the little things right, don't expect to do the big things right". This can apply to so many different parts of our lives, but let's look at it at its face value.

Do you think the successful people of the world wake up late, live in a sloppy house, and don't follow through on their promises? Do you think the millionaires of the world hit the snooze button 10 times and show up two hours late to work? Do you think world-class athletes skip their workouts to binge fast food and watch Netflix? Do I even need to answer these questions? Most of the time, we know the right answer to our problems. Unfortunately, it's not always the easy answer or the thing we want to do. But I promise you that just a small sacrifice of short-term satisfaction will pay exponentially in long-term fulfillment and gratification.

Consistency

Consistency is continually showing up time and time again, even when you don't see results. Consistency is trusting the process over a long time before you reach the goal. It is very hard to stay consistent, but it is one of the most important things to do if you want to achieve true success. You must try again and again, even if you fail every single time. However, we must try not to consistently do the wrong things. Consistently change up your angle and tackle your problems from a different vantage point. Keep throwing shit at the wall until something sticks, but switch up your plan of attack while you remain consistent.

You are the only one who will change your life. No one is going to do this for you. So, you need to be the one who holds yourself accountable. You need to be your own parent and make yourself do the things you don't want to do. In order to achieve long-term success, you need to sacrifice short-term satisfaction.

Please don't be too hard on yourself to the point that you're doing more harm than good. We all get down on ourselves sometimes but don't stay there. We all make mistakes and fail. Pick yourself up and try again. In most situations, half the battle is just showing up consistently. Everything in your life will require consistent work. Even after you have "made it," your life will still require consistent maintenance. Success is a marathon, not a sprint. Pack up for the long journey.

Getting Up Makes You Mentally Stronger

Your mind is like a muscle. Just like when you go to the gym to work out your chest, biceps, and legs, you must exercise your mind by making healthy choices. You can callous your mind with dedication and the attitude of never giving up. The repetition of healthy habits and being strong mentally will slowly sharpen your mind and change the way you think. Treat your brain like a muscle and work it out by making the right choices and creating the right habits. Just like when you go to the gym, overtime you will get stronger and the exercises will get easier.

When I was 19 years old, I had to shut down my first business. For the past few years, I had owned a company called Conquer Your Cart. It was an Amazon store that sold groceries, toys, and home items. Long story short, I had to shut it down. I had failed the business I had been running for years. I was very lost, to say the least. I didn't know what direction to take my life, so I went nowhere. I got lazy, developed bad habits, and slowly went into a downward mental spiral. I didn't know what to do. This resulted in me doing nothing at all.

Eventually, I came to start my second business. A YouTube channel. But I didn't jump right into it. I slowly had to pick myself up and keep moving forward regardless of the failures in the past. Using momentum and the little successes I had, I gained the confidence to keep pushing. In order to pick myself up, I would start with a very small task. Something like doing the laundry. That small success would give me the boost of energy I needed to do another and then another. Even the small successes would give me the strength to keep pushing.

I had to learn how to reprogram my mind. I did that by taking the little wins and running with them. Getting up and pushing, the actual act of action, motivated me to keep going. Get up, gain momentum, and push through. The hardest part is the start. If you find yourself in a tight spot like I was, focus on doing the little things right, and use your small wins to motivate you to keep going. Take your mind to the gym.

Momentum

We rarely feel 100% ready, 100% motivated, and ready to go for the day. Your day and your attitude are never going to be absolutely perfect, and you will never be READY to start living your dreams. If you wait for the perfect moment, you will end up waiting until you die. The perfect moment does not exist. People often wait for the exact time to start a business, get in shape, or ask that person out on a date. The truth is that a perfect time will never come, and you will never be 100% ready for anything. The key, is to just do it anyways.

Doubt and fear will kill more dreams than failure ever will. We let so many subconscious things hold us back from doing everything in life. It robs us of our future. I'm trying to say that if you have a goal or a dream, just go for it. One of the hardest things to do is get up and start doing it. I promise you that it gets better and easier. Some of the scariest failures are those we create in our minds to convince ourselves not to go for it.

You will never be in the exact right mood or right setting to pursue your goals. But momentum and action are the most important parts of achieving a goal. Action and momentum serve to motivate you and push you even further. You do more because you do more. When I work hard, I'm only inspired to work harder. Pushing through things and keeping going also brings up our self-esteem. This comes back to the morning routine, and that's why momentum is so important.

Winning the morning can either be my biggest advantage or downfall. This one hits me pretty hard. Having a morning routine is one of the most important pieces of my daily momentum. If I do not win in the morning, I feel awful for the rest of the day. A structured morning routine mentally prepares me for the day.

Let's look at a day filled with momentum and one without momentum. When your alarm goes off bright and early, it is your job to ignite the momentum for the day. If you can win the morning, you can win the day. Getting up early is arguably the most important decision you will make in the day. Let's say you succeed, which you will because you are awesome and you work hard.

You get up early and hit the gym. You're happy, proud of yourself, and you feel good, so you want to eat a good breakfast. I literally have the urge to eat healthier foods when I act healthier and make healthier choices. I have never once left the gym after a morning workout and had the crippling desire to gorge my body weight in donuts. So, you got up early, worked out, and decided to eat a healthy breakfast. There's no reason to stop now because you feel good. You take this good attitude off to work or school and you get lots done and embrace your productive habits. Habits compound, and they compound exponentially. Both good and bad.

Now, let's look at a day with negative momentum. You sleep in through your multiple alarms. You finally get up, and you're late for work. You don't have time to eat a healthy breakfast, and you really don't feel like it, so you pick up some fast food on the way to your job. The food doesn't make you feel great, but it's something in your stomach. You're not on the ball for the day because you don't feel prepared and didn't take time for yourself mentally and physically before you start the day.

Therefore, your work suffers, and you don't perform as well as you would have liked. You get down on yourself because you don't see good results. So, you treat yourself with activities that only soothe the pain and don't actually fix it. Because you were not proactive, you don't feel great by the end of the day and are by no means encouraged to do better tomorrow. Your self-esteem has fallen, and you are upset with yourself.

I have gone through both of these days many times, and every single time, sacrificing the short-term satisfaction of sleeping in pays off in the long run for providing me with a healthy, happy, productive day. Personally, there is an extreme difference in my life when I lead the day with positive momentum as opposed to negative momentum.

Sometimes at our lowest points, our emotions and our mind are all out of whack. So, we need to rely on what we know to be true and what we know to be right. Momentum can serve as a backbone of our mental health and productivity. I use momentum to make myself feel better and get back into the swing of things when I'm having a bad day.

Let's say I sleep in late and feel bad about myself. I know that getting up and doing things will make me feel better, so I try to make it easier for myself. I give myself a very small task to get me out of bed and start the momentum. Get up and brush my teeth. OK, that wasn't so hard. While I'm here, I might as well put my contacts in as well. OK, even just doing that little bit made me feel better. I think I'm going to take a shower. Wow, I feel a little better now. Maybe I'll do something easy, like throw in a load of laundry. These tasks keep getting bigger and bigger while the momentum builds. The more you do, the more you continue to do.

This was one of the biggest, if not the biggest, things that helped me get out of a depressive state. Just taking little baby steps and compounding from there. We all want to hit the ground running, but sometimes all you can squeak out is a baby step. That's exponentially more beneficial than doing nothing.

DON'T GIVE UP

When The Going Gets Tough

This will be the hardest thing you have ever done. It will probably be one of the greatest challenges that you face. But after the long haul of your journey, the payoff will be greater than anything you have ever received before. You will FEEL so much better once you embark on this journey. You will face tough times, but if you get tougher, they will pass.

Maybe you're stuck, or you found yourself in a situation where you don't really know what to do. Maybe you don't exactly know how to react. Maybe a new challenge has thrown itself into your life. Unexpected things will happen to everyone. Thankfully, there's a process for that. The first thing you want to do is understand that whatever situation you are in, you can overcome it. The second thing you should understand is who you are. All of your core values will bring you through your challenging times.

Life will smack you in the face, bring you to your knees, and keep you down if you let it. At this point, it's up to you to use your knowledge to move forward. Analyze your situation. How did you get there? What went wrong? What mistakes did you make? Once you can pinpoint how things went wrong, you can usually determine what caused that sudden change.

Maybe you strayed from your values, or maybe you lacked experience. Maybe it wasn't even your fault. But it's your responsibility now. Pinpoint the problem, understand your situation, get up, and keep moving forward. Before you start this journey to your dream life, I want you to understand that it is tough. It will be hard. It will strain your mind and body and push them past their limits. It will be challenging, but it will also be worth it.

When It's Time To Start

Getting started is the hardest part. Getting up and going is the first big hurdle to doing anything great. I'll admit, that big goal you have can be intimidating. Sometimes we want to shy away from pursuing that dream. Maybe we are scared of failure, what others will think, or just feel overwhelmed. For those reasons, we do nothing at all and avoid starting the journey. The truth is, the worst thing we can do is nothing at all. Your goal may be risky, but doing nothing guarantees you will not achieve it. Getting up is the only way to give yourself a fighting chance. You need to start.

It can be tempting to put off that dream or idea you have. Maybe you are pushing your dreams back because you're "just not ready yet," or "the business isn't quite ready to launch," or "I'll wait till the new year to start going to the gym." If you wait till you are "ready" to start something, you will wait forever. The truth is, you will never be fully 100% ready for anything. The big secret is to just do it anyways. Recently, I heard someone say "If you're not embarrassed about your first product, you launched too late." I really thought about this when writing this book. I did not want to publish it too late.

During the process of writing this book, I started by creating a list of different topics I thought where important. Then, I spoke about these topics on my laptop. Then, I reviewed the spoken words, edited, and reformatted them to make everything sound smooth and fix errors. Then, it will get sent off to a professional editor and published. I am tempted to re-read this book ten times and rewrite every sentence to sound as best as possible. But this book will never be perfect; if I strive for absolute perfection, it will never get done. I would rather have a published book that is 95% perfect than a book that never made it off my laptop. I can always come back and create a volume two if I want to, but I would rather put out something than nothing. Even if it isn't perfect.

The circumstances will never be perfect for you to start working on your goals. The stars will never align 100%. You will never feel like doing it every day, you will never have enough time. Just go! Stop waiting for the right moment and start doing the thing you want to do!

Most people throw in the towel way too early. It's not over till it's over, and it's not over until you win. You are not being held back by your age. You are not being held back by anything except for that thing between your ears. You don't have to wait till you're out of school, you don't have to wait till you're 40, you don't have to wait till after college, you don't have to wait at all.

Let's put this into an example. Let's say that you are a 16-year-old kid in high school, and your dream is to start your own business. You want to take the traditional route of high school, then college, then start your business. Roughly, you will be 22 by the time you leave college after a four-year degree and enter the real world. This is around the age that most people start working. If you were that 16-year-old kid and your dream was to start a business, start now!

There is nothing actually holding you back. Imagine how much knowledge and experience you will have under your belt by the time most people start their life. At age 22, when you are leaving college and getting a job, most people will have zero years of work experience in their chosen field. At 22, you will have six solid years of business experience. Imagine how much knowledge you have compared to everyone else who is starting at Ground Zero. You have failed many times, learned so many times, and grown through the process years ahead of everyone else. You can learn a hell of a lot in six years, and there is absolutely nothing that should be holding you back. The sooner you start something, the better.

Not Just One Thing

Striving for greatness will make you feel good. After you get over that hump of starting the task, it feels better. Economically, the best thing to do is usually specialize and then outsource. That means focusing on one thing and outsourcing everything else. However, being a relatively rounded person will provide you with many benefits. A true hero tries hard at everything. OK, cool, you're a millionaire now, but your marriage sucks, you're a jerk to your kids, and you struggle with addiction. A truly great person does well in all aspects of life, or at least tries.

Changing your life and habits will allow you to be great in all categories. True successful people are successful physically, emotionally, mentally, and financially. Some say that the four pillars of life are health, wealth, love, and happiness. I believe that for us to be complete, we must work hard in all categories. No, you won't be good at everything. I sure am not. But I take comfort in the fact that even if I try something new and fail. I at least gave it a pretty dam good shot.

It's Not Over

You are never out of the fight. NEVER. You can always come back to be great no matter how dark it may seem. Maybe you dropped out of college, got fired, or lost that relationship. It is never too late to go back to school, it is never too late to go for the job you want, and it's never too late to love again. The only thing that is holding you back is your mindset.

So many people act like your life is over at the age of 40 or 50. Are you 40 years old? You've got a good solid 40 years left, at least. Don't just give up on your life halfway through. This also applies to people in their 20s and 30s. You can do nothing from age 20 to 30, and still be fine. You're young; you can make mistakes and, most importantly, learn from them. You can never go back and relive those opportunities.

The most depressing and painful feeling of all is the feeling of regret. The painful feeling of wishing you would have gotten up. It's not too late. It's never too late to at least try living your dream life. The person who tried and failed has my respect 100X more than the person who wonders what if. We are not going to be here forever. Make the most of it.

EXPONENTIAL SUCCESS

Becoming the Type of Person That Gets the Goal

What does achieving your goal look like? What type of person has what you want? What do they do on a daily basis? How do they eat? How do they act and treat others? How do they spend their time? In order to achieve what you want, you need to become the type of person who has that thing.

It's not even about the goal. It's about the person you become along the way. Sometimes, we don't have what we want in life because we have not become the type of person that has that thing. Think again about that confident, dedicated, successful person. That person displayed all of those traits before they became successful. They had to become all of those things before they achieved the success.

Achieving the dream is an amazing accomplishment. But it's not the most important aspect of changing your life. The most important aspect of changing your life is becoming the right type of person along the way. It's not about the goal. It's about becoming the type of person that achieves that goal. It's about turning into the man or woman you need to be to live your dream life.

There will always be another mountain, another goal, or another accomplishment we are trying to achieve. It's about the journey of continued improvement. Once you reach that goal, seek more. More growth, improvements, and impact. You should be proud of your accomplishments and how far you've come. You will get to a point in your journey where you look back and don't even recognize the person from the beginning. A quote I love goes "Always grateful, never satisfied". We should be proud of our accomplishments, but the journey is never over.

Speaking to Me

I am not perfect. I will never be. But it is in pursuing perfection that I find value in my life and experiences. Everything in this book I fully believe. Most of the time, when I write, I am speaking to myself. All of the topics in this book are challenges I have been through and will probably go through again. Hopefully, you and I can both use these experiences to help us overcome the next challenge we face. I don't want you to get the wrong impression. Just because I wrote this book doesn't mean my journey is even close to complete. The journey of self-improvement is one that never ends.

Not everything in this book will resonate with you. We all have our own things that inspire us and drive us to do better. What motivates me probably won't motivate you. Everything we do on our journey to living our dream life will differ for each person.

However, there are many common struggles we all face. Learning how to overcome the struggles can help us reach our destination, no matter our journey. When I write these chapters, I am talking to myself. All of the things in this book I am also telling myself. Most of the time, when I talk about the subjects or try to explain them, I talk myself through the challenge. You just happen to be reading my thoughts in this book. I am trying to give all this advice to me. I do this because I have dealt with all of the challenges in this book and, using all of the methods I explained, worked through those challenges.

Will everything in this book work for you? No. You choose what experiences you can draw from and which ones you want to disregard. But that goes for all of life. Once you find out where you are going. The path that you are on. You can choose how to use the knowledge and experiences you have acquired over the years.

Compounding Success

Everything in this book has the potential to change your life for the better. But when life starts to get crazy, you combine many of these principles to create a hardened warrior of a human. Individually, everything in this book will help you succeed. But if you combine these things, you can become unstoppable, and your growth will be exponential. Mastering one area of life will help you master the other. Maintaining a healthy body will bleed over into maintaining healthy relationships, and that can bleed over into maintaining healthy finances. It all compounds together, and it all works to make us better at every angle.

We should all strive to be better at everything we do. There is no point in being rich if you haven't managed happy relationships in your life. It is counterintuitive to be successful in one area but toxically lacking in another. On the path to success, many people often let their health slide. But this is such a missed opportunity. Becoming financially wealthy while maintaining a healthy body will make you exponentially stronger and smarter than the person who only has one. You need money to be healthy, and you need to be healthy to make money. The more money you have, the more time you can buy, and the more time you have, the better you can take care of the relationship between your family, kids, or lover.

Let's go over an example. I want to be financially successful. I'm sure many of you reading this book do too. Reaching that goal of financial success or financial independence will open the doors for so many other goals of ours. After many long years, we finally reach our goal of being financially successful. Congratulations!

Now, we want to take on a new goal. That goal is to publish our very own novel. Writing our own book can be very time-consuming and cost money. But, because we succeeded in our first goal, to be financially successful, we have made it much easier to accomplish this second one. Now, we can afford to take extra time off work to write. We can afford to hire the best editor to review our book for us. We can also use our financial success to get rid of all the things we don't want to deal with in our lives. That way, we can spend our time achieving our new goal.

This is part of why successful people seem to get so much done. They can use their success and prior achievements to make them even more successful. Being successful in one area can inspire you to be successful in another, and it also makes it a lot easier. You can do anything. You can succeed on multiple levels. That's when the real fun starts.

Keep Moving Forward

Most of the time, I literally have no idea what I'm doing. I do new things all the time. I second-guess almost everything I do. I'm even second-guessing writing this book right now. Almost all of the things I try, I'm unsure if they will work out. I don't know much of anything. Regardless, I keep moving forward. It's very easy to get stressed about life and especially overwhelmed. It happens to me all the time. But the truth is, nobody has it 100% figured out. We all have fears, we all have self-doubts, and we all second-guess ourselves. I have an idea of where I'm going in life, but life changes and evolves as you move on through it. Please don't let your fears or lack of knowledge hold you back.

Putting our heroes and idols on a pedestal can be very easy. But they really are no different from us. It's easy to think that they have it all figured out. But we only see their successes. We see the team winning the championship all over tv, but we don't see the countless hours in the gym practicing. We see our favorite actor on the big screen, but we don't see the years and years of practice leading up to the roll.

All of us, even our heroes, struggle with the same feelings we do. Greatness is in every single one of us. No one in a position of success has gotten there without paying their dues. You don't have to have life figured out to realize that greatness. You just have to keep moving forward. Move forward through doubt, fear, pain, anxiety, depression, or whatever else life can throw at you. Life will figure out a way to throw everything at you. This life will put you through the ringer. But you can't lose sight, and you can't lose focus. Action is the only thing that can physically bring you closer to your goals. Keep moving forward.

My Journey

I have written extensively in this book about my personal experiences and the common traits of successful people. But I never shared what my own personal journey to success is. My personal goals have changed and molded throughout the years as I try to pivot in an out of good and bad situations. I still have mostly the same overall goals, but how I plan to get there and my path changes. Growing up, I knew from a very early age that I wanted to be in business. I wanted to be a businessman and an entrepreneur. I wanted to own multiple businesses, be financially smart with my money, and own a large investment portfolio. Going through school, I tried to take up practical skills to help get me there.

I graduated college with a double major in accounting and finance. I knew that college wouldn't teach me much about owning my own business, but I thought that learning accounting and finance could help. So right now, as my day job, I work as an accountant. I'm not ecstatic about my work, but I take home an average salary that pays the bills for now. A stable job can offer some benefits like access to credit and health insurance that my own business does not.

I understood the vision and the idea of what I wanted from a young age, but I didn't really know how to get there. When I was 19 years old, I hit a pivot point. I had failed big many times in my life. I didn't get into the college I wanted to, that one hurt really bad, and I had to close down my first business. I owned an Amazon store where I would resell and wholesale various products from my area. So, I was pretty lost. I didn't know what to do, where to go, or how to start a new business. So, I just started moving forward as best as I could.

I grew up in Detroit. I've always been really interested in cars, entrepreneurship, business, and fitness. So, I decided to start a YouTube Channel alongside the things I like. I've gone through many changes in my channel, but I want this to serve as a way for me to document my journey and share my passions. My idea was that I was already going to these car shows, starting businesses, and doing these things. The only difference was that now I have a camera with me. This was also a fun way for me to share the things I loved. Over the years, I changed and molded my style, but I have been growing my business ever since.

This next part is sort of a business plan I wrote myself for my life. I wrote this when I was struggling to see the bigger picture and frustrated with my lack of progress.

This is how I have laid out my path moving forward. It goes "Youtube Plan: create a community of people that enjoy my channel by sharing my experience. This platform is used to funnel multiple businesses through and then use profits to invest. Why? Because I pledge to be successful in the community, which I admire. I promise the money is worth it, work for yourself and no one else. It is worth it, but you need to keep going in order to realize that worse. The only way this will work is if you want it bad enough. You need to want this dream so badly that it hurts you not to get it. I sometimes feel discouraged because I have put in all the work and time without any return, but all the struggle will make the success much better. I am an entrepreneur with a passion, love, and the knowledge of a businessman and investor. I am a creative mind, and with the proper combination of these skills, I can create an extremely successful and dangerous combo.

I have learned so much on this journey; it is only getting started. I have to remind myself of the rules and ideas in this book all of the time because I struggle with every single one of them. On the path to success, we can all expect to grow and change and mold into the type of person we need to be in order to get the goal. I am by no means a massive success. I have tried lots of times, and I have failed lots of times. But in this book are some of the lessons I picked up along the way.

Because of the principles in this book, I have been able to take action and take control of my life. I march closer and closer to my goals every day. I know I will achieve my goals. I know that you will too. I find myself getting overwhelmed looking ahead at the big picture and all of the goals and dreams I have. In times like that, it is important to remember to keep moving forward and just focus on one thing at a time.

I would very much like to hear your story and your journey to living your dream life. Below are all my social media accounts if you want to reach out or just follow along for the journey.

Youtube: Caylebpletos

Instagram: Caylebpletos

TikTok: Caylebpletos

After This

I wanted to take a second to thank you personally for reading this book. It would mean the world to me if you could leave this book a review to help share it with more people. If you have any questions or concerns, you can always reach out to me on any of my social media. I would be more than happy to chat with you. There are many books in the world; you chose to pick up this one, and I very much appreciate it. I hope it was able to help you, and I wish you lots of luck on your journey to success. Anything you want to achieve in life is already inside of you. You just need to find a way to bring it to the light. Now go take everything that you have learned and put it into action! You can do it! I believe in you!